PROJECT
KID

CRAFTS THAT GO!

PROJECT KiD
CRAFTS THAT GO!

AMANDA KINGLOFF

Author of *Project Kid*

60
Imaginative
Projects That
Fly, Sail,
Race, and
Dive

ARTISAN
NEW YORK

Published by Artisan
A division of Workman Publishing Co., Inc.
225 Varick Street
New York, NY 10014-4381
artisanbooks.com

Published simultaneously in Canada by Thomas Allen & Son, Limited

Library of Congress Cataloging-in-Publication Data

Names: Kingloff, Amanda, author.
Title: Project kid : crafts that go! / by Amanda Kingloff.
Description: New York : Artisan, a division of Workman Publishing Company,
 Inc., 2016. | Includes index.
Identifiers: LCCN 2016012873 | ISBN 9781579656836 (pbk.)
Subjects: LCSH: Models and modelmaking—Juvenile literature.
 Handicraft—Juvenile literature.
Classification: LCC TT157 .K4372 2016 | DDC 745.5928—dc23 LC record available at http://lccn.loc.gov/2016012873

DESIGN BY YEON KIM
ILLUSTRATIONS BY JORDAN SONDLER

Printed in China
First printing, August 2016
10 9 8 7 6 5 4 3 2 1

For my mini-makers,

Oliver
&
Sommer

CONTENTS

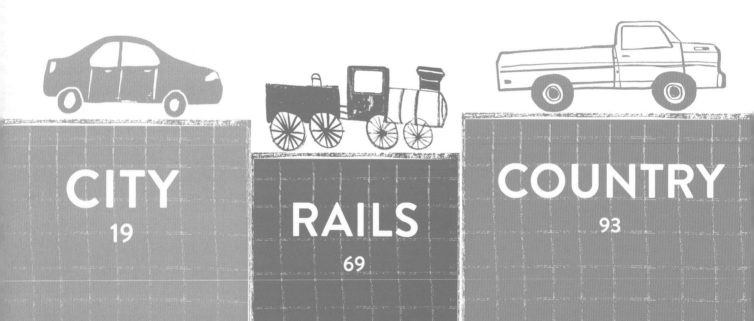

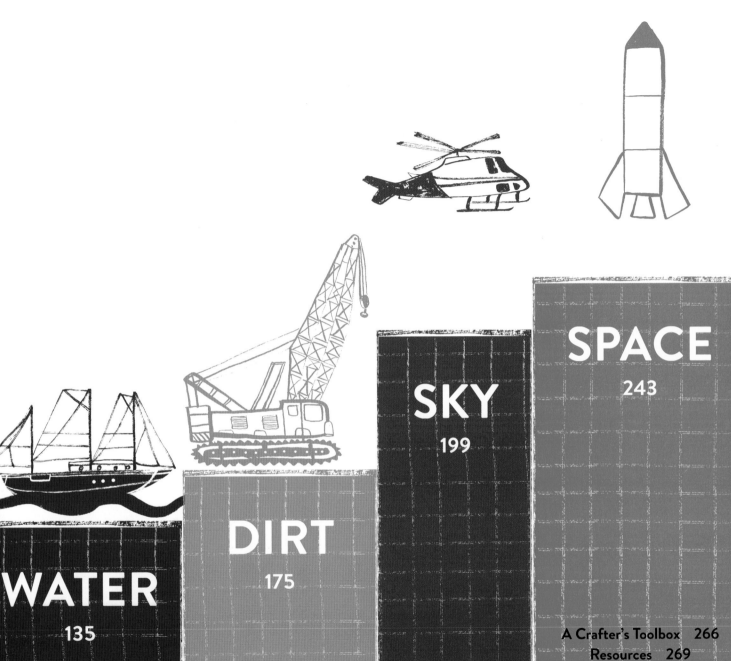

Foreword

When Amanda's first book, *Project Kid: 100 Ingenious Crafts for Family Fun*, was introduced to the world, it was no surprise that families from New York to Zanzibar raved about the endless hours of unplugged time crafting and making that the book inspired.

Now Amanda takes Project Kid on the road, in a new book filled with super-cool transportation-themed crafts. She will lead your children on an imaginary journey into the deep blue sea and fly them to the moon. They will skywrite with a paper airplane, build construction vehicles from cardboard, and engineer found objects into submarines. These surprising and satisfying projects will no doubt inspire conversations about inventors and visionaries who dreamed big and succeeded!

You'll be super impressed by the mantel-worthy creations from even the tiniest makers. Amanda's purposeful design of each project guarantees that every boy and girl will have success. Step-by-step photos will help beginning readers and visual thinkers feel confident about working independently through the book. We of course expected nothing less from a mother of two who has delivered creative content to millions of parents for more than a decade.

We're giving *Project Kid: Crafts That Go!* five glued and glittered gold stars!

High five,
Jonathan & Rachel Faucett
HANDMADE CHARLOTTE

Introduction

This book was born out of my son Oliver's love for all things that go. Ever since he could walk and talk, he has wandered into my craft room and said those words any maker mom loves to hear: "Mommy, I wanna make a project." And when I ask what he wants to make, the answers—a helicopter, a plane, a train, a race car, a submarine—always have one thing in common: he wants to make something that *moves*.

If you know even one kid, you know that at a very early age, children develop interests that can accurately be described as full-on obsessions. Some go for princesses, others dinosaurs, but it's the beloved transportation category that captures the imagination of every kid, from water babies to outer-space explorers. This book was created for them. For every child who has ever laid his little head on the rug to watch the wheels of his train chug slowly along the tracks. For the kid who flies her plane around the living room, dodging lamps and bookshelves to land it safely on the dining room table. And for the one who can make the perfect *vroom* and *screech* sounds for his superfast race car.

But this book is not just about making toys that go. Tailor-made for the fanatical kid, it's an all-encompassing, immersive crafting and educational experience for children who just can't get enough of vehicles and the environments in which they are found. Within these seven chapters, you will find playful decor, costumes, accessories, and tons of pretend-play projects that you can make with and for the children in your life. As you flip through the pages, you'll discover "blueprints" that teach kids the proper terms for the major parts of a train engine, submarine, rocket ship, and more, so that when they get to a project, they'll not only craft a vehicle but also understand that they're creating a car's wheel axles or a ship's mast.

As I crafted these sixty projects, I ran them all by my live-in five-year-old editor, Oliver. His opinion mattered 100 percent. If he was bummed out because a car was missing a hood ornament, I would figure out a simple way to include one. If I failed to disguise an upcycled item properly, he'd call me out on it. But when I nailed it, he would twitch impatiently, needing to make that vehicle right then and there. And that was when I knew the project was a winner—when it was not just that he wanted to *play* with something I had made, but that he wanted to *make his own*, riffing on my original, transforming it into his unique invention. That was my signal of success, and that is what fills these 272 pages. I hope you enjoy making these crafts as much as we have. (And if you have a problem with any of them—take it up with my editor!)

Material World
CRAFT SUPPLIES 101

One thing I've heard from parents over and over again is that part of what makes crafting intimidating is all the *stuff*. There are so many options, brands, and types of materials! Don't stress; if you have these sixteen things in your arsenal, you're off to a successful start.

1. **Cardboard:** Don't throw away that cereal or FedEx box. It will come in handy, I promise!

2. **Felt:** A great fabric for beginner crafters because it comes in a variety of shades, it's sturdy, and when it's cut, the edges don't fray.

3. **Scrapbook paper:** Traditionally sized in 12-inch-square sheets, scrapbook paper comes double-sided, solid, textured, patterned, holiday-themed . . . you name it, they make it.

4. **Kid scissors:** Have a bunch of these on hand for playdates and birthday parties.

5. **Hole punch:** Imperative for garland making, DIY lacing cards, and all things hole-y.

6. **Hot-glue gun:** An adults-only tool that creates an instantaneous strong bond; the best cure for impatient crafters who are allergic to drying time.

7. **Tacky glue:** A great all-purpose adhesive that's stronger than school glue but safer than hot glue.

8. **Glue dots:** Quick, clean, and kid-friendly, they come in different strengths, from repositionable to permanent.

9. **Colored masking tape:** Rip-able, thick, and affordable for striping or covering large areas.

10. **Paint:** Have a mix of tempera, watercolor, and acrylic on hand for your young Picassos.

11. **Foam paintbrushes:** Very inexpensive; can take a beating from the youngest of makers.

12. **Mod Podge:** A necessity for any decoupage project.

13. **Yarn:** Soft and affordable; comes in many weights and textures.

14. **Wood craft sticks:** A classic, useful building block for many, many projects.

15. **Beads:** They can always be added to embellish a simple project.

16. **Buttons:** Good for eyes, wheels, headlights, and the centers of flowers.

Flip to A Crafter's Toolbox (pages 266–268) for a more in-depth look at the whats and whys of craft supplies.

WHEELS

In the pages that follow, there are *a lot* of wheels. In the interest of variety, I did my best to . . . um . . . reinvent the wheel whenever I could. But if you don't have the right button or washer or coaster called for in a specific project, do not fret! Behold these craft and household objects that can all become *wheely* perfect wheels.

plate

plastic lid

tape roll

plastic lid

bottle cap

napkin ring

washers

rhinestone

cedar hanger ring

bangle bracelet

reflector

tag

cork lid

beads

cork coaster

jar lid

Cabone ring

embroidery hoop

plastic lid

bottle tops

ball jar lid

bottle cap

cork stoppers

jar lid

spool

grommet

wood circles

buttons

FLYING GEAR

The craft potential of rotors, wings, and propellers is vast. If you don't have a perfectly shaped material, just bend wire or ribbon to suit your needs.

ribbon

spatula

spoons

wire

plastic toy flyer

GoGo Squeez applesauce pouch cap

spoon

pipe cleaner

Popsicle sticks

ice cream spoons

tongue depressor

wavy craft stick

ROADS

While you're making your own vehicles, you may want to craft the streets, runways, and dirt roads on which they will travel, too! (Parents, this extra touch may help you to avoid airplanes landing on your antique dining room table.) Go thin or wide, black or brown, dashed or lined—and the longer, the better!

ruler

belt

tape

yoga mat

ribbon

cardboard

How to Craft with Kids

Crafting is not just about the result; it's about the playful and inventive journey of getting there. The search for materials, the improvisation when something doesn't go according to plan, the conversation that ensues when a mini-world is being created—all of these things add texture and richness to this unplugged time with kids.

All makers need to explore in order to get inspired. Whether you go on a walk in the park, to the hardware store, or to the supermarket, help your kids to see the world as their craft store. Collect rocks, sticks, pinecones, and acorns from the backyard. Explore the little drawers in your local hardware store, full of nuts, washers, and doodads that baffle even you. Study the different shapes of drink bottles at your local corner store.

Sometimes it's the juxtaposition of things that creates a new idea. Maybe your son notices a bright-red car parked by a yellow house—and suddenly you have a color scheme for your next project. Perhaps a leaf is lying at the tip of a stick and your daughter sees this as a magic fairy wand. Or maybe a soccer ball shooting down the field makes your kids think of a game they want to build with marbles.

Crafting is invention, and all inventions have a backstory. Ask questions about what you are making together. What is this vehicle called? What's the destination of this car, plane, or boat? How many people can fit in this vehicle? What happens when it needs repairs? Encourage a story that might lead to a companion project.

Allow children to take a step out of their comfort zone, their everyday environment, in order to see the world and its parts in a different way. And who knows . . . the trip may inspire you too.

A NOTE ON SAFETY: I make it a point not to add age ranges to my projects, because all kids develop at different speeds. Many of these projects can be scaled up or down to suit your child's age. Nonetheless, be aware of what is safe for the kids with whom you are crafting.

Tools like hot-glue guns and utility knives should be used only by adults and should be kept off the main crafting area. (I like to keep my glue gun plugged in on the kitchen counter where my kids can't reach.)

If you have little ones crawling around on the floor, be mindful of any dropped buttons or beads that could be potential choking hazards.

DIT: DO IT TOGETHER

I've never heard a kid say, "I can't do that; I'm not crafty." But I hear it from parents ALL. THE. TIME. If you're one to freeze up in the aisles of the craft store—or while holding this very book in your hands—you are not alone. But I promise, you can do this. Here are a few morsels of practical advice.

Decide on a craft location and keep your supplies where you craft. Whether it's your kitchen table, your basement, or your playroom, designate a destination creation station. Once you decide on where you'll be crafting, find a nearby drawer or shelf that can be repurposed to keep your supplies. Consider investing in clear plastic bins with snap-on lids. You can group your paints, embellishments, and tools together, respectively, and skip labeling the bins (this is also useful for your pre-reader children).

Let the mess happen. Invest in a "splat mat," a plastic tarp, or rolls of butcher paper to protect your floor. And then accept that things *will* get messy. Your floor will get wet. A paintbrush cup will tip over. And you will find dots of glitter on your skin for weeks. But trust me, the benefits will silence your inner neat freak. While you're crafting, fight the urge to clean up until the end—and make cleaning up part of the process. Maybe the butcher paper that caught all the drips and spills will become the most beautiful thing you made that day.

Take creative license. Let kids make their projects their own—even if the projects are coming from a how-to book with nitpicky instructions. Throughout this book, you'll see that I've called for materials in specific colors and sizes; but oftentimes that's just to help you see how the materials function in the project.

Remind your kids (and yourself) that there are *no rules* when it comes to aesthetics. And I give you permission to simplify projects! It's okay if you don't add that origami boat to the shadow puppet theater on page 152 or the pom-pom fringe to the hot-air balloon on page 234. Feel free to omit embellishments, add them later, or come up with your own . . . that's the fun in it all!

Break free of the refrigerator door. Many of the projects you'll find on these pages can't be held up with a magnet. Your kids want to see what they've made living on a wall or shelf in their home. It will encourage them to create more and will fill them with a great sense of pride.

CITY

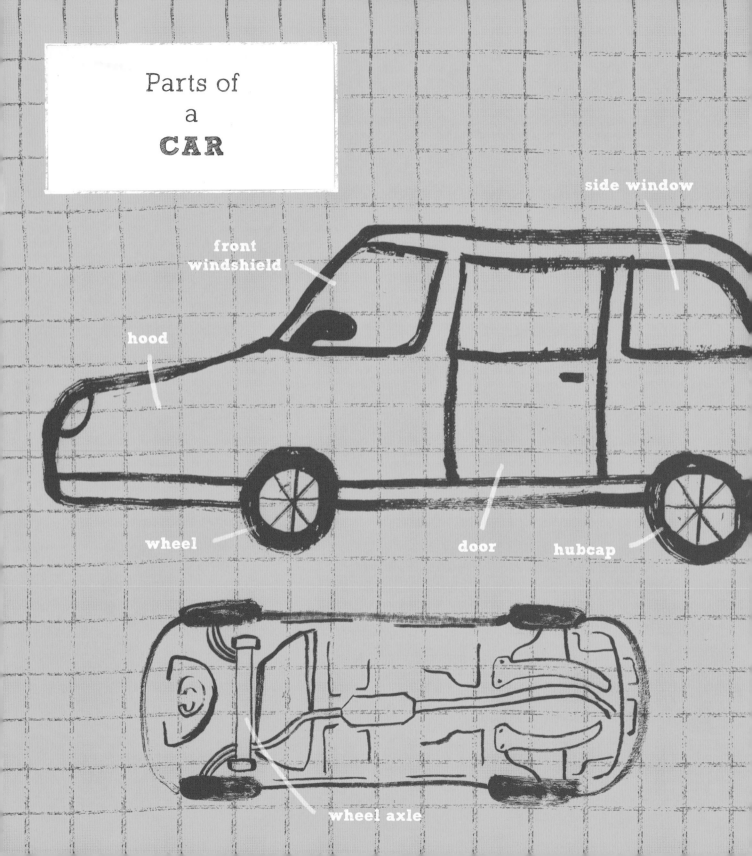

Parts of
a
CAR

side window

front
windshield

hood

wheel

door

hubcap

wheel axle

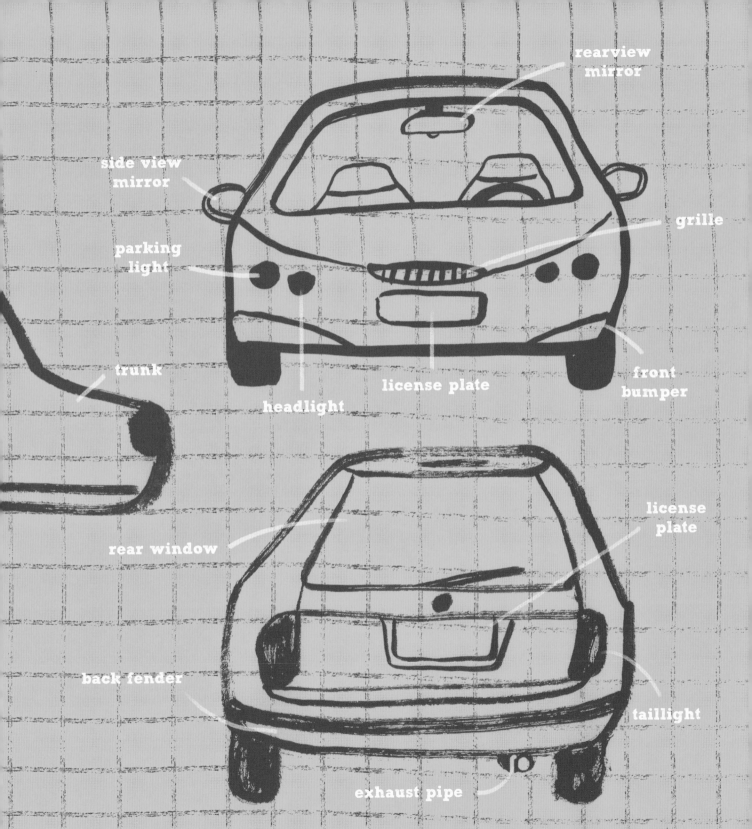

rearview mirror

side view mirror

grille

parking light

front bumper

trunk

license plate

headlight

rear window

license plate

back fender

taillight

exhaust pipe

JEWELRY-BOX CAR

Never throw out a gift box! Make compact vehicles with earring boxes, and limos and 18-wheelers with watch boxes.

WHAT YOU'LL NEED

- 2 jewelry boxes in different sizes
- Tacky glue
- Washi tape in various colors, including blue and silver
- 4 shirt buttons (2 yellow and 2 red)
- 1 cardboard food box
- Scissors
- 2 wooden skewers
- Four 20 mm disk beads (available from Etsy.com)
- 4 small wooden beads
- ⅛-inch hole punch

1 Glue the smaller box on top of the bigger one, open side down. Decorate both with washi tape. Use blue tape for the **front windshield**, **rear window**, and **side windows** and silver tape to create the **front bumper** and **back fender**.

2 To make the car's **headlights**, glue the yellow buttons to the front of the car on either side of the bumper; to make the **taillights**, glue the red buttons to the back on either side of the fender. To make the car's **grille**, cut the bar code from the cardboard food box. Trim to about ½ inch tall and just wide enough to fit in between the yellow headlight buttons on the front of the car and glue in place.

3 To make the **wheel axles**, trim the skewers to measure about 1 inch longer than the width of the box. (If you score the skewers by just barely cutting into them with scissors, they will snap cleanly when you break them.) Now add the **wheels**: slip two disk beads onto a trimmed skewer, then glue a small wooden bead to each end of the skewer. Repeat with the second skewer.

4 While the wheel axles are drying, punch four "half holes" in the bottom edge of the box (inserting the edge only halfway into the punch) about ½ inch from the front and back of the car on both sides. Glue the wheel axles into these notches.

ROAD COASTERS

Create your own city, over and over again!

WHAT YOU'LL NEED

- Blank square coasters (available from Amazon.com)
- 1-inch-wide black masking tape
- Yellow electrical tape
- Scissors
- Pencil
- Blue and green paint
- Paintbrushes
- Adhesive Velcro (optional)

1   To make a straight section of road, stick a piece of black tape in the middle of a coaster. Cut three thin strips of yellow tape and stick them on top of the black tape as the dividing lines.

2   To make a corner section of road, mark the middle point on the edges of two adjacent sides of the coaster and center two strips of black tape on those marks. Trim to a right angle where they meet in the middle of the coaster. Cut three thin strips of yellow tape and stick them on top of the black tape as the dividing lines.

3   To make water, paint coasters blue; to make grass, paint them green.

4   To prevent slippage when playing with these tiles on carpet, adhere a square of the bristly side of adhesive Velcro to the back of each coaster.

To create a fully operational city, make about twelve straight road pieces, twelve corner pieces, and eight each of the grass and water pieces.

DRY-ERASE STREET SIGNS

Become a junior city planner and design your own street signs. Turtle crossing? Why not!

WHAT YOU'LL NEED

- 1¼-inch and 2-inch or 2½-inch wooden circles
- Dry-erase peel-and-stick wall decal (available from Staples.com)
- Pen
- Scissors
- Wooden skewers
- Hot-glue gun
- Red, black, and yellow dry-erase markers

1 Trace either the 2-inch or 2½-inch wooden circle onto the dry-erase decal and cut out. Peel off the back of the decal and adhere to the wooden circle.

2 Cut a skewer so that it's 3 inches long. (If you score the skewer by just barely cutting into it with scissors, it will snap cleanly when you break it.) Have an adult hot-glue the non-dry-erase side of the large wooden circle along one end of the skewer. Apply a pea-sized amount of hot glue to the center of the 1¼-inch wooden circle and glue the bottom end of the skewer into it, holding it in place until the glue is dry, so that the sign can stand up by itself.

3 Use dry-erase markers to create your street sign.

4 Repeat steps 1 through 3 to make as many signs as you'd like.

Did you know that the upside-down equilateral triangle is exclusively used for yield signs? And that only the stop sign uses an octagon shape?

FIRE TRUCK LAMP

Extinguish this light just by flipping a switch!

WHAT YOU'LL NEED

- One 1-by-5-by-4-inch wooden planter box (available from JamaliGarden.com)
- Twelve 2-inch wooden blocks
- 1 extra-long paint stirrer
- Six cedar hanger rings (available from BedBathandBeyond.com)
- Red, white, and black paint
- Paintbrushes
- Tacky glue
- Silver drawer liner or silver bubble wrap
- Scissors
- Yellow ribbon
- Black felt
- 4 red beads
- 2 thimbles
- Six 1-inch white buttons
- Hot-glue gun
- 1 battery-powered lightbulb lamp (available from DCIGift.com)
- 10 yellow zip ties (available from HomeDepot.com)

1 Get all of the painting out of the way first. Paint the outside of the planter box and eight blocks red, four blocks and the paint stirrer white, and all of the cedar rings black.

2 Once the blocks are dry, glue the red blocks into one large cube and then glue the four white blocks on top to make the truck's cab.

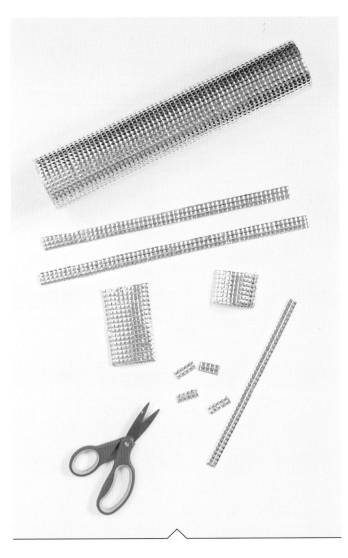

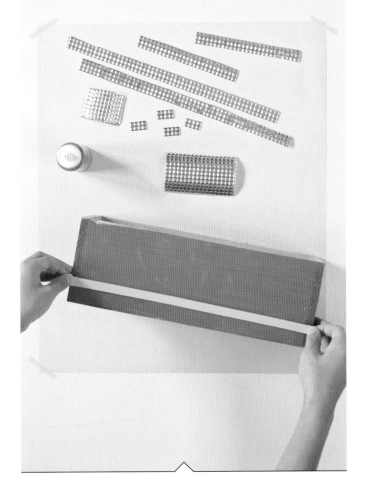

3 Cut the silver drawer liner to the following measurements: a 32-by-½-inch strip (or strips) to go all the way around the truck as a bumper; a 3-by-2-inch strip for the side control panel; a 2¼-by-1½-inch strip for the grille; and four ½-by-¾-inch pieces for the headlights.

4 Cut two 11-inch pieces of yellow ribbon and glue them horizontally about 1 inch up from the bottom of the truck on both long sides. Glue on all the silver pieces as shown in the photograph on page 31.

Cut five pieces of black felt: four 1¼-inch squares as side windows and one 3¼-by-1¼-inch rectangle as the front windshield. Glue these in place on the white blocks.

To make the truck's lightbars (or beacons), glue the red beads in a row on top of the white cab of the truck, and glue the thimbles just behind and to the side of the red beads.

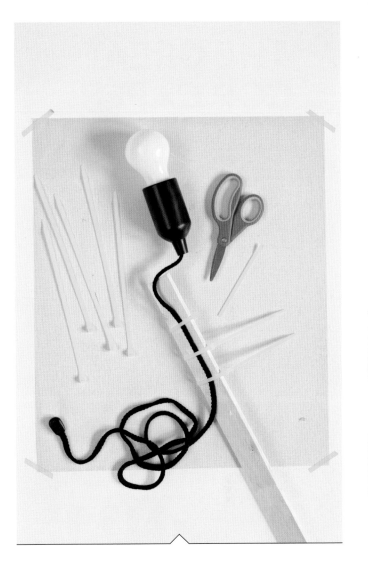

 To make the truck's wheels, glue a white button in the center of each of the cedar rings. Mark the center point of each ring and then have an adult hot-glue the rings to the sides of the truck, with two in the back and one in the front on each side, lining the center marks up with the bottom edge of the truck to make sure it's stable.

Lay the lamp cord over the paint stirrer and secure it to the stirrer using approximately ten zip ties, spaced about 1 inch apart. Trim the ends of the ties. Place the cab in the front of the box and rest the ladder/light from the back bottom edge of the truck bed on the cab. To secure, have an adult add a generous line of hot glue to the bottom of the stirrer.

THE GREAT COP CAPER

This police car is full of pretend-play potential, from munching on plush doughnuts to issuing speeding tickets in the living room.

WHAT YOU'LL NEED

- One 40-by-60-inch piece of ¼-inch-thick foam core
- Utility knife
- Black paint
- Paintbrush
- Silver duct tape
- Hot-glue gun
- 5 plastic cups: 2 red, 2 blue, and 1 clear
- Tacky glue
- Black paper
- Light colored pencil
- 2 yellow sponges
- Blue painter's tape
- Scissors
- Black masking tape
- Black 3-inch letter stickers
- Doughnut and coffee (optional)

You can set the police car in front of a chair or, to create a stand, use duct tape to attach two large right triangles cut from foam core to the back of the car, behind the wheels.

POLICE

1. To make the body of the car, have an adult cut a foam core rectangle measuring 26 by 32 inches with a utility knife, rounding the corners slightly.

2. To create the **front windshield**, have an adult cut another rounded-corner rectangle that measures 12 by 24 inches. Cut the rectangle into a trapezoid by slicing off a small piece of foam on each short side. Out of that rectangle, cut away the "window," leaving a frame that's 3 inches wide. Have the child paint the frame black. Once it's dry, use duct tape to attach it to the back of the large foam core rectangle.

5. To make the **headlights**, trace a sponge onto black paper and then cut out that shape, making it about ½ inch wider and longer than the outline. Repeat for the second light. Glue the sponges to the black paper then the black paper to the foam core, about 3 inches above the bumper.

6. To make the **grille**, adhere five horizontal strips of black tape in between the headlights, graduating the lengths and cutting them on the diagonal to create a trapezoid shape. The shortest strip should be about 11 inches and the longest 16 inches.

3 Have an adult cut a 3-by-15-inch piece of foam core, plus two 3-inch right triangles. Hot-glue the triangles to the top right and left corners on the back of the windshield and then glue the 15-inch piece on top of them as a ledge. The child can then use tacky glue to attach the cups to that ledge to make the flashing lights.

4 To create the **front bumper**, have an adult cut a 34-by-3-inch piece of foam core and let the child cover it with silver duct tape. Add a horizontal strip of blue painter's tape in the center of the silver strip. Have an adult hot-glue the bottom edge of the bumper about 4 inches from the bottom of the front of the car.

7 Spell out POLICE with the letter stickers, about 2 inches above the grille.

8 To make the **wheels**, have an adult use a utility knife to cut two 5-inch-square pieces of foam core and round one edge on each. Have the child stripe them with black tape, leaving tiny white lines in between to create tire treads. Use duct tape to attach the tires to the back bottom corners of the car, about 2 inches in from each side.

LEARNER'S PERMIT

Give your kids license to drive (their scooters) with these Shrinky Dinks ID cards.

WHAT YOU'LL NEED

- Shrinky Dinks ink-jet paper (available from Michaels.com)
- Computer and ink-jet printer
- Scissors
- Washable markers
- Parchment paper
- Cookie sheet

1 Print a 3-by-3-inch photo of the child on the printable Shrinky Dinks paper, justified to the left side of the paper.

2 Cut a 4-by-7-inch rectangle out of the paper, positioning the photo toward the left middle section of the rectangle. Round the rectangle's corners.

3 With markers, let the child write his name, eye color, hair color, age or birthday, and state of residence on the rectangle.

4 Place on a parchment-covered baking sheet and then place a piece of parchment paper on top of the license and bake in the oven according to package instructions.

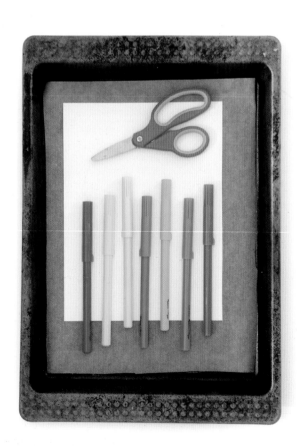

OLiVeR

NEW York 5

SOMMER

NEW YORK 3

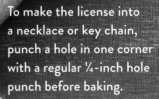

To make the license into
a necklace or key chain,
punch a hole in one corner
with a regular ¼-inch hole
punch before baking.

BEJEWELED HEADLIGHT PURSE

Step on the gas, but don't drop this clutch!

WHAT YOU'LL NEED

- Car template (download at ProjectKid.com/purse)

- Computer, printer, and printer paper

- Scissors

- One 18-inch-square piece of felt

- Pen

- ¼-inch-wide silver ribbon

- Tacky glue

- Silver sequins

- Two 1-inch-diameter buttons

- 6 rhinestones: two ½-inch clear, two ⅜-inch yellow, and two ½-inch red

- 1 small cardboard box (about 3 by 5 inches, like an animal cracker box)

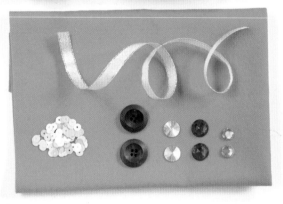

This purse was designed to mimic the style of the 1950s Fiat 500. Did you know that this car is less than 12 feet long? You could line three of them up in a row, and they would still be shorter than a school bus!

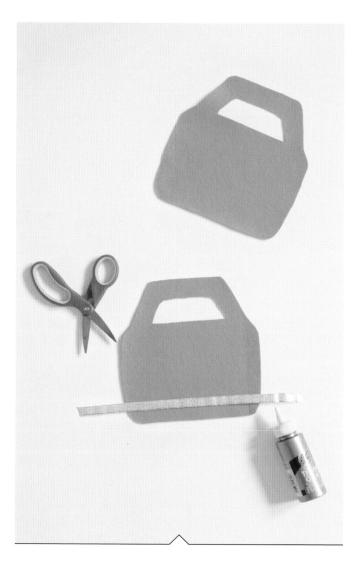

 Download and print the car template, cut it out, and trace it onto the felt twice. Cut out the felt.

To make the car's **front bumper**, cut a 7-inch piece of ribbon and glue it across one piece of felt, about 1 inch up from the bottom. Fold any excess ribbon around to the back of the felt and glue the ends.

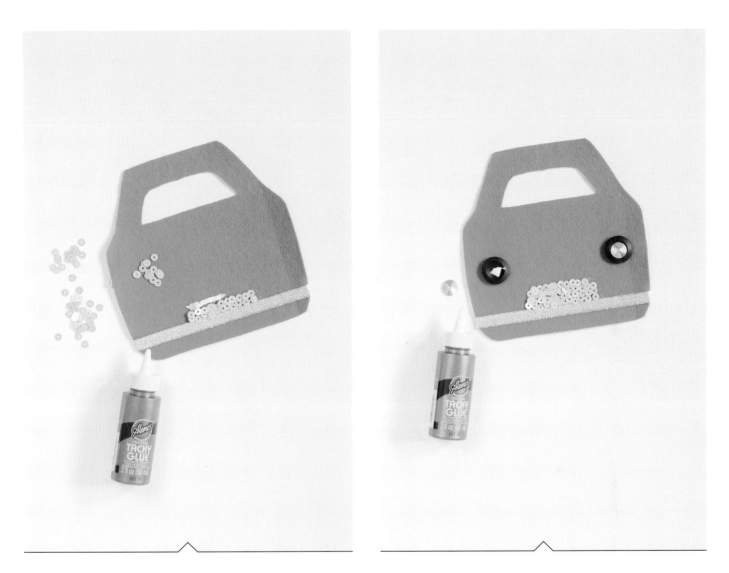

To create the car's **grille**, glue four rows of sequins in a 3-inch trapezoid-like shape, centered just above the bumper.

To give the car **headlights**, glue the buttons about 1½ inches above the bumper and about ½ inch in from either side. Glue the clear rhinestones on top of them.

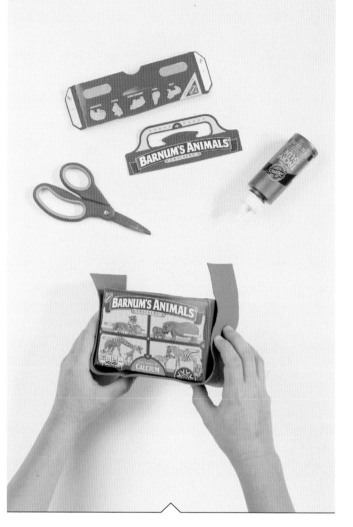

 Add the car's **parking lights** by gluing the yellow rhinestones just below and on the outside of the button headlights.

 Cut a strip of felt that is as wide as the depth of the box, and long enough to wrap around two short sides and one long side. (A standard animal cracker box needs a 12-by-2-inch strip.) Glue the felt strip to the side and bottom edges of the cardboard box, leaving the large sides blank.

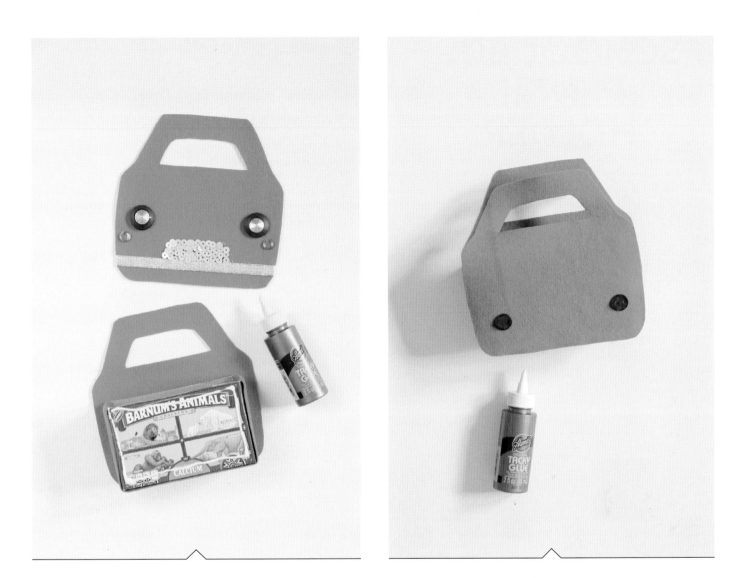

 Glue the blank felt piece to one large side of the box, and glue the undecorated side of the first piece of felt to the other.

 To make the car's **taillights**, glue the red rhinestones to the back of the purse.

SCHOOL BUS PENCIL HOLDER

Leaving your scissors, pencils, and markers in this school bus is no cause for alarm!

WHAT YOU'LL NEED

- One 3-inch-square cracker box (mine was a Stoned Wheat Thins box)
- Yellow paint
- 2 paintbrushes: 1 thick and 1 thin
- 1 small jewelry box
- 2 small yogurt cups
- Pencil
- Scissors
- Hot-glue gun
- Chalkboard paint
- 4 Cabone rings (available from Michaels.com)
- Black yarn
- 4 red thumbtacks
- 2 silver snaps or buttons
- Black permanent marker

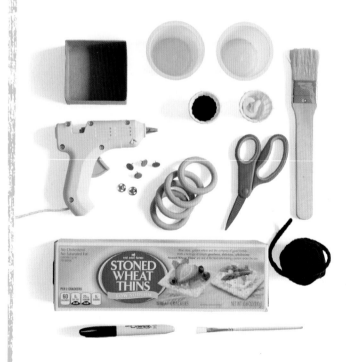

 1 Unfold the cracker box and paint the inside yellow. Paint the outside of the small jewelry box yellow (set aside the lid—save it for another project). Let both dry.

2 Trace the open ends of the yogurt cups about 1 inch apart on one side of the box. Have an adult use scissors to puncture a small hole inside each circle and let the child cut the shapes out (staying about ⅛ inch inside the line).

3 Restore the cracker box to its three-dimensional shape with the yellow side showing, and have an adult hot-glue it back together. Insert the yogurt cups into the holes you cut on the roof (if your cups don't have a lip to hold them in place, stuff some newspaper underneath for support). To make the bus's hood, glue the jewelry box, open side down, to the bottom half of one of the short sides of the cracker box.

4 Paint six windows on each side of the bus; paint two doors, the front windshield, and a front bumper onto the bus with chalkboard paint (refer to page 49 for placement). The bus windows should be about 1 inch square and the doors about 1 inch wide by 2½ inches tall. The windshield should cover most of the area above the hood, leaving just a slim yellow frame. To make the bumper, paint a thin black stripe along the bottom, open end of the jewelry box.

 To make the bus's wheels, paint the Cabone rings in chalkboard paint and let dry.

 Have an adult hot-glue one end of the yarn to the ring. Wrap the yarn around each ring, turning the ring to create an asterisk wheel pattern. After four to five wraps, cut the yarn and have an adult hot-glue the loose end to the ring. Hot-glue each wheel about 1 inch in from the front and back of the bus on both sides.

7 Add the brake lights and parking lights by pushing two red thumbtacks into each corner above the windshield (secure with a dot of glue if needed); to make the headlights, glue the snaps on the bumper.

8 Draw the bus's grille by making three horizontal marker lines on the front of the hood, just above the bumper (see page 49). Draw two horizontal lines along each side of the bus, under the windows.

STOP, SLOW, GO!

Just turn the dial on this homemade stoplight to play red light, green light . . . or control the traffic in your living room!

WHAT YOU'LL NEED

- 1 large cracker box (the size that saltines come in)
- Scissors
- 1 large shoe box
- Black and yellow paint
- Paintbrush
- 1 wrapping paper tube
- Pencil
- Hot-glue gun
- Red, yellow, green, and black scrapbook paper
- Glue stick
- 1 tall Pringles can

The first gas-powered traffic light was installed in London, England, in 1868. Before that, policemen stood in the street to direct traffic!

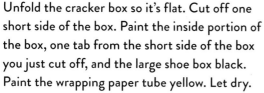

Unfold the cracker box so it's flat. Cut off one short side of the box. Paint the inside portion of the box, one tab from the short side of the box you just cut off, and the large shoe box black. Paint the wrapping paper tube yellow. Let dry.

Draw three 2¼-inch-diameter circles (you may use a small Play-Doh lid as a template) evenly spaced down one side of the cracker box. Have an adult use scissors to puncture a small hole on the edge of each circle and let the child cut them out. Put the circles to the side. Fold the box back into a three-dimensional shape with the black side showing and have an adult hot-glue it back together.

 To make the light shades for the traffic signals, fold one of the cutout circles in half and cut three slits from one edge to the fold. Curve the circle a bit so that the painted sides bends down slightly, place the cut edge of the circle along the top inside edge of one of the circle openings, and have an adult hot-glue the slits to the inside of the box. Repeat for the other two circles.

4 Cut out a 9-inch-square piece of black paper. Cut 3-inch squares from the red, yellow, and green paper. Glue the red square to the top left corner of the black paper, the yellow square exactly in the middle, and the green square in the bottom right corner. Draw "emoji" faces on the colored squares, if you wish.

5 Glue the black square of paper around the Pringles can, with the red square nearest to the closed end of the can. Cut a 4-inch strip from the box scraps and fold in half. Bend the ends outward to form a T shape, and glue the ends to the closed end of the can as the turning dial.

6 Have an adult use scissors to puncture a small hole in the bottom center of the cracker box. The child can then use the scissors to cut six ½-inch slits outward from the hole in an asterisk-like shape. Push the wrapping paper tube through the slits and have an adult secure the tube inside the cracker box with a generous amount of hot glue at the seam.

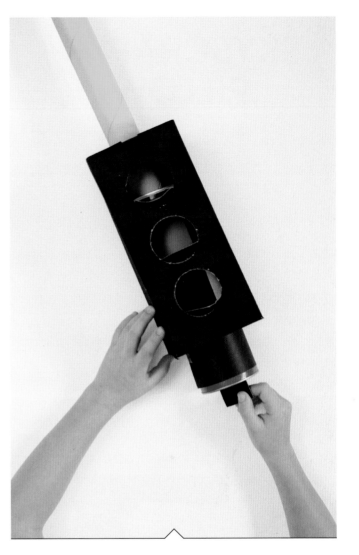

 Use the cutting technique used in step 6 to create the same-sized hole in the center of the shoe box.

 Push the wrapping paper tube down into the box until it hits the floor, and then have an adult secure the tube inside the shoe box with a generous amount of hot glue at the seam. Drop the Pringles can down into the top of the cracker box so that it rests on the tube.

SKYSCRAPER PILLOW

Graphic and bold, this easy-to-make throw pillow can double as a backdrop for imaginative play.

WHAT YOU'LL NEED

- Throw pillow
- Scrap paper
- Scissors
- Black and yellow felt
- Fabric glue

1 Begin by making a rough layout of your window grid on the pillow using rectangles of scrap paper. You can let your little architect figure out how big he wants his windows to be; the green pillow shown here (from Pier1.com) fit thirty windows that were 2½ inches tall by 1½ inches wide.

2 Once you have a design you're happy with, cut rectangles from black and yellow felt. Cut one yellow rectangle for approximately every five black.

3 Lay out your window pattern on the pillow, interspersing yellow windows as you go. Glue the felt windows to the pillow, making sure you apply the glue to the outermost edges of each rectangle. Let dry for at least an hour before reclining.

PINT-SIZED ICE CREAM TRUCK

Here's the scoop: while making this project may require a lot of grown-up help, it will be worth it for all the ice-screams!

WHAT YOU'LL NEED

FOR THE TRUCK

- 1 file box (mine was part of the Tjena series from IKEA)
- Utility knife
- Hot-glue gun
- 1 magazine file (mine was also part of the Tjena series)
- Washi tape in various colors
- Scissors
- Scrapbook paper, solid and patterned
- 4 thick cork coasters (available at IKEA)
- Four 2½-inch-diameter wooden circles
- Pencil

FOR THE ICE CREAM CONE

- Mint, pink, and cerise honeycomb paper (available from Devra-Party.com)
- Scissors
- Glue dots
- Brown butcher paper
- Cookie cooling rack
- 1 wooden skewer
- Tacky glue
- Brown crayon

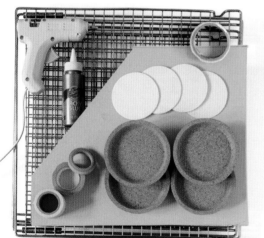

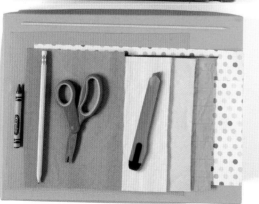

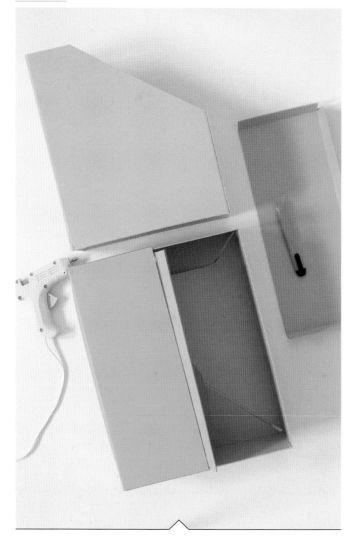

1 Have an adult cut the file box lid in half with a utility knife and hot-glue one half to the box. To make the shelf for the serving window, cut a 4-inch-high-by-13-inch-wide strip out of the remnants of the lid. Fold in half lengthwise and have an adult hot-glue one half to the inside edge of the box. Hot-glue the magazine file and file box together, with the magazine file opening pointing toward the left and the open file box on the right. The bottom edges of both boxes should be flush.

2 Let the child decorate the truck: Stick a horizontal strip of washi tape across the center of the side of the truck. Add vertical strips of tape from this center line down to the bottom of the truck, spacing them about an inch apart. Cut a window shape from scrapbook paper and use washi tape to attach it to the "door" of the truck, above the center line.

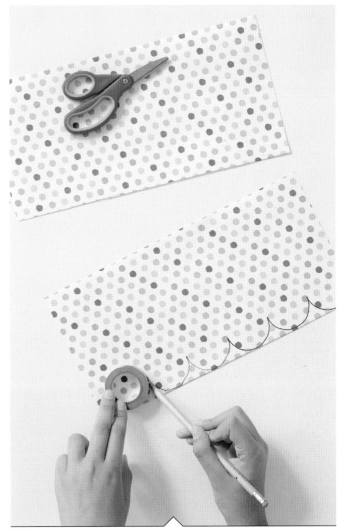

3 To add the wheels, have an adult hot-glue the cork coasters about 2 inches from the front and back ends of the truck on either side. Have the child use thin strips of washi tape to create an asterisk-like shape on each of the wooden circles. Have an adult hot-glue one circle to the center of each cork wheel.

4 To make the awning: Cut a piece of scrapbook paper in half. Lay a roll of washi tape (about 2 inches wide) along the 12-inch edge of the paper and trace. Repeat so you have about six circles drawn edge to edge across your paper. Cut out the scalloped edge. Align the straight 12-inch awning edge with the back edge of the top of the truck and have an adult hot-glue in place. Fold the scalloped edge of the awning down across the front edge of the truck.

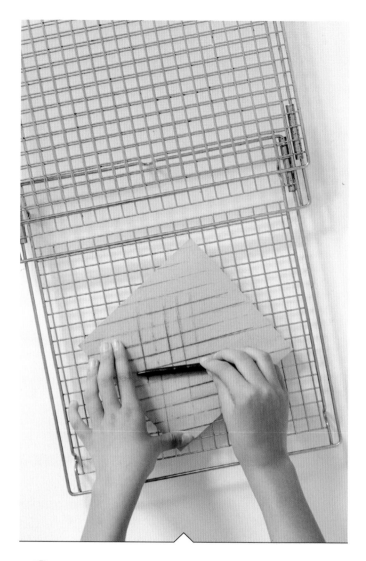

5 To make the ice cream scoops, trace two 3-inch semicircles in each of the three colors of honeycomb paper. (You can use a small jar lid as a template.) Cut out. Fan out the paper and use glue dots to attach the flat sides of each half-sphere together to create a sphere— one for each color.

6 To make the cone, cut a 6-by-6-inch piece of butcher paper. Lay the paper on a cookie cooling rack and rub with a peeled brown crayon. Turn the paper 90 degrees and rub again, creating a waffle pattern.

7   Roll the paper into a cone and secure with the glue dots. Trim the top of the paper cone to get a straight edge.

8   Insert a skewer into the center of the three ice cream scoops and down into the cone. Add a dot of tacky glue in between the three scoops and between the bottom scoop and the cone to secure it onto the skewer. Add a line of tacky glue to one side of the cone and affix to the top of the truck, if you wish.

RAILS

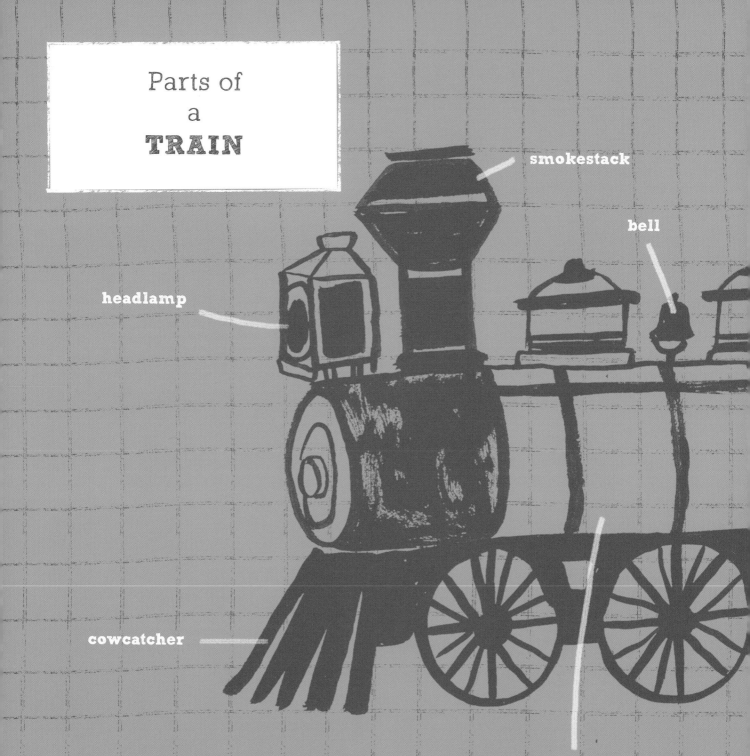

Parts of
a
TRAIN

smokestack

bell

headlamp

cowcatcher

boiler

cab

cab window

crankshaft

wheel

ALPINE MOUNTAIN TUNNEL

Take your toy train on a brisk ride through a homemade mountain range.

WHAT YOU'LL NEED

- Two 12-inch-square pieces of cardboard
- Pencil
- Utility knife
- 4 matching pieces of 12-inch-square scrapbook paper
- Scissors
- Glue stick
- White felt
- Tacky glue
- 1 oatmeal container
- Hot-glue gun
- Gold washi tape

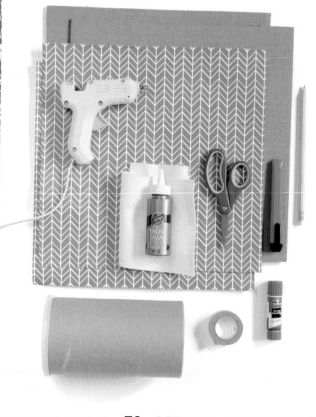

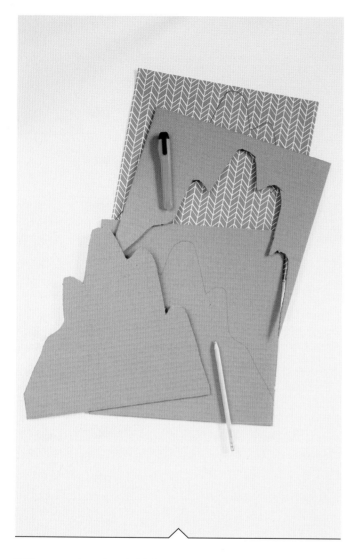

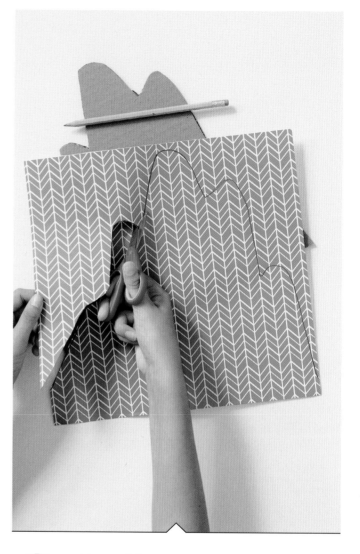

Let the child draw his mountain shape on one piece of cardboard, then have an adult carefully cut it out with a utility knife. Trace the first mountain onto the second piece of cardboard and the four sheets of scrapbook paper, making sure to flip the cardboard when tracing the two back sides of the mountain.

As an adult is cutting the second mountain out with the utility knife, have the child cut the scrapbook paper shapes with scissors.

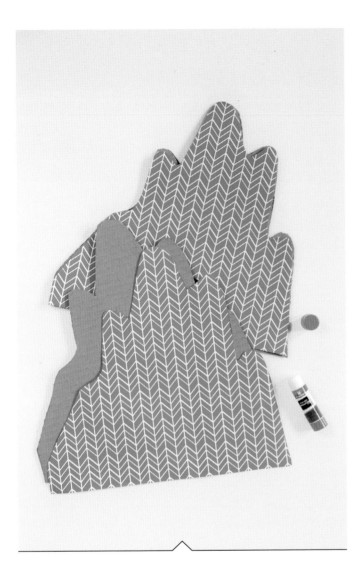

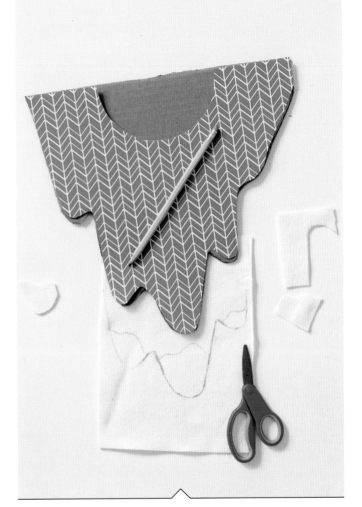

3 Use a glue stick to adhere the mountain-shaped scrapbook paper to the cardboard.

4 Trace the peaks of each mountain onto the white felt and then draw onto the felt small snowdrifts that just top the mountains. Cut these out and glue them to the mountaintops with tacky glue.

5   To make the tunnel, peel the outer label from the oatmeal container, cut the container in half lengthwise, and trim off the closed end so that the tunnel is about 5 inches long.

6   Trace the semicircle opening of the oatmeal container onto both pieces of cardboard, centered along the bottom edge of each mountain. Have an adult cut the semicircles out of the cardboard with a utility knife.

Have an adult hot-glue the tunnel to both sides of the mountain and hold in place until the glue is set.

Rip about fifteen 2-inch-long strips of gold washi tape and stick around one tunnel entrance, folding and sticking them inside the tunnel. Repeat on the other side.

RAILROAD CROSSING MAGNET

When your little conductor sees this project, he might down that jar of olives just so he can get crafting!

WHAT YOU'LL NEED

- One 2½-inch black metal jar lid
- Yellow paint
- Paintbrush
- Black tape
- Scissors
- Black ½-inch letter stickers
- Mod Podge Dimensional Magic
- 1 magnet
- E-6000 glue

1 Paint the inside of the jar lid yellow and let it dry. Apply a second coat if needed.

2 Cut two pieces of black tape, about ⅜ inch wide by 3 inches long. Stick them down on top of the dry yellow surface in an X formation.

3 Stick one uppercase "R" on each side of the X shape, centered in the yellow wedge.

4 Using even movements and slowly working your way over the surface of the lid, fill the lid with Dimensional Magic. Be careful not to create bubbles. Let dry for at least 3 hours undisturbed.

5 Have an adult glue a magnet to the back of the lid with E-6000 glue and let dry completely before using.

GROWTH TRACK(ER)

Track your children's growth as they travel through childhood.

WHAT YOU'LL NEED

- Two 5-foot-long, 1-by-2-inch oak planks
- 60 Popsicle sticks
- Black and white acrylic paint
- Paintbrushes
- Painter's tape
- White pencil
- Measuring tape
- Wood glue
- Six 1-inch wood circles
- ¾-inch number stamps
- Red ink pad
- 2 small D-rings
- Hammer
- 2 screws to suit your wall
- 1 red tongue depressor
- Clothespin
- Washi tape

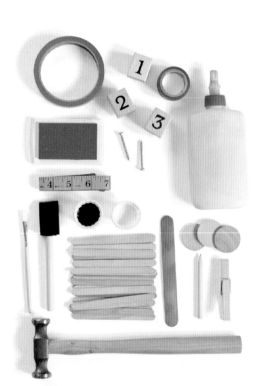

1 Paint the oak planks and one side of each Popsicle stick black. Let dry.

 2 Lay the oak planks on the floor, skinny side down, 2¼ inches apart. (Use painter's tape to secure them to the floor at each end so they can't move.)

 5 Stamp numbers 1 through 6 on the wood circles. Let the ink dry before handling.

 6 Glue the "1" circle to the very first rung. Have the child count up twelve rungs, to the point where he should glue the second foot marker. Continue until you reach 6 feet.

 **9** To make the railroad-crossing gate, paint white diagonal stripes on the red tongue depressor. Once the paint is dry, glue it to one flat side of the clothespin, lining up one end of the tongue depressor with the pinching end of the clothespin. Use this to mark the height of your child on the corresponding railroad tie.

 **10** Use the washi tape to mark children's heights on the wall. Write their names and ages on the tape.

Starting at one end of each plank, make marks every inch with a white pencil.

 Glue a Popsicle stick across the two planks at every inch mark. Let dry, undisturbed, for 30 minutes.

 Once the glue is dry, flip over the growth chart and have an adult hammer the D-rings into the top back side of each rail.

 Measuring so that the bottom of the growth chart is 1 foot above the ground, insert the screws at the point where the D-rings hit the wall and hang the chart from them.

SUBWAY GLOBES

For the city transit lover, these New York City subway globes are a surefire hit (as sure as those pesky train delays).

- 6- to 14-inch-diameter paper lanterns in the colors of the MTA subway lines
- Pencil
- White paint (or black, if using a yellow lantern)
- Paintbrush
- String or twine
- Scissors
- Ceiling hooks

1 Draw the letters or numbers of the trains on the paper globes and fill in with paint.

2 Cut a piece of string and tie it to the top of the lantern. Make a loop with the other end of the string and hang the lantern from a ceiling hook. Repeat for the other lanterns.

All New York City subway signage uses the famous Helvetica font. To make your globes as authentic as possible, you can create your own Helvetica stencils: Print out each letter or number in this font, sized to fit your globe. Then cut out each one, trace it onto the lantern, and fill in with black or white paint.

SASSY CIRCUS TRAIN

Step right up and craft a toy to hold plastic animals from a box that used to hold edible ones.

- 16 pieces of wagon wheel pasta (rotelle)
- Resealable sandwich bag
- Hand sanitizer
- Yellow and red liquid food coloring
- Parchment paper
- 5 animal cracker boxes
- Scissors
- Yellow paint
- Paintbrush
- Duct tape in various colors
- ¾-inch permanent dot stickers (available in 52 colors and patterns from InStockLabels.com)
- Adhesive Velcro
- Permanent glue dots
- 21 miniature wooden Popsicle sticks
- Enamel dot stickers (available from Michaels.com)
- 2-inch-tall spool
- 2 straws
- 4 plastic coffee stirrers
- Tacky glue
- Thin string
- Small animal toys (about 3 inches tall)

BONUS PROJECT:
Paint plastic animal figurines for a more modern big top.

1
Shake the pasta pieces in a resealable bag containing a teaspoon of hand sanitizer and about 3 drops of yellow and 1 drop of red food coloring to dye them. Shake until coated and lay on parchment paper to dry.

2
Cut off the front side of three of the animal cracker boxes, leaving about ¾ inch on the bottom intact. Paint the insides of the boxes yellow.

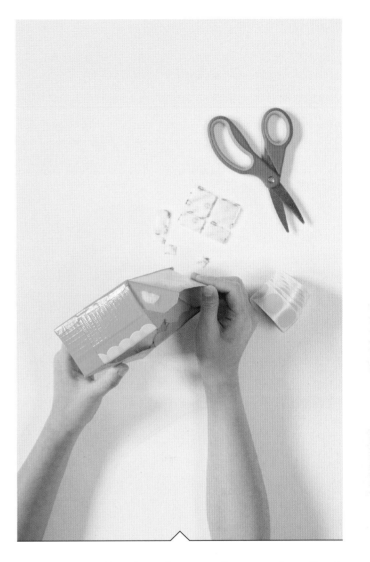

 3 Cover the outsides of these three boxes with duct tape, folding the excess tape inside the box. Do not seal the top edge—you want to be able to lift the lid to get the animals into and out of their cages.

4 Fold circle stickers over the open edges of each box to create a scalloped border around the cage opening. Where the box opens at the top, cut and adhere a small piece of Velcro at each flap so that it stays closed when the animal is inside.

5 Use glue dots to secure the wooden sticks to the inside edge of each car, seven per car.

6 To make the **train engine**, cut about 3¼ inches from one end of the lid of an unused box so that the other unused box can rest vertically inside of it. Cover both boxes together in duct tape. Cut four ¾-inch squares of another color of tape for **cab windows** and a 1-inch square for the front windshield. Add a stripe of contrasting colored tape along the bottom of the engine. Fold circle stickers over the bottom edge of the box to create a scalloped design and add enamel dot embellishments.

To make the **smokestack**, wrap a piece of duct tape around the center of the spool and attach it to the front of the engine with a glue dot.

To add the train's **wheels**, turn each car upside down and glue two 2-inch straw segments to the bottom of each car, parallel to the front edge, about 1 inch from each end. Insert 3-inch-long pieces of the coffee stirrers into the straws, put a pasta wheel on either end of the stirrer, then seal with an enamel dot sticker and tacky glue. Cut a 24-inch piece of string and tape to the bottom of the train cars, spacing them about ¾ inch apart.

COUNTRY

❋

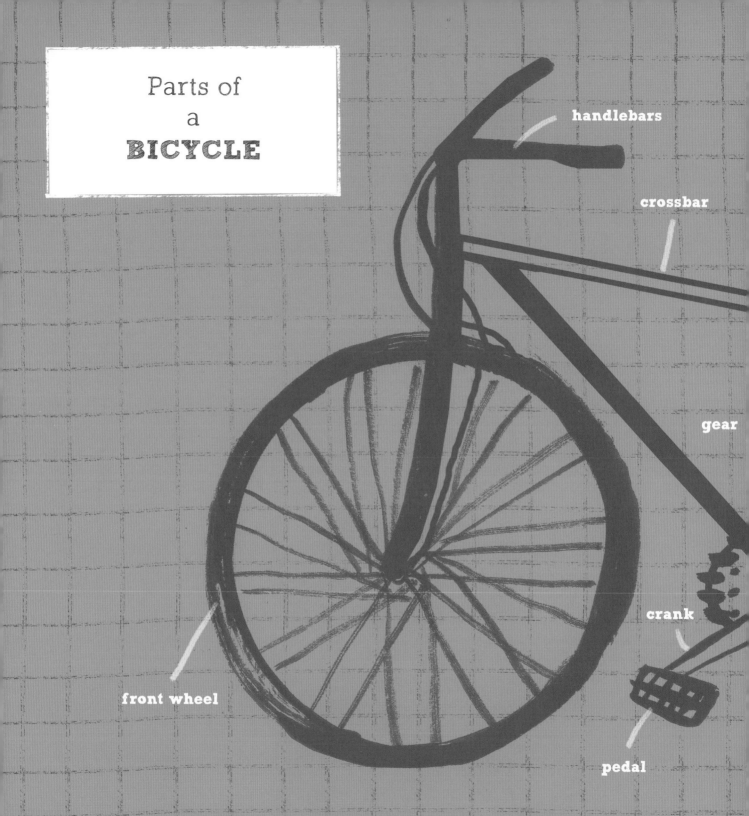

Parts of a **BICYCLE**

handlebars

crossbar

gear

crank

pedal

front wheel

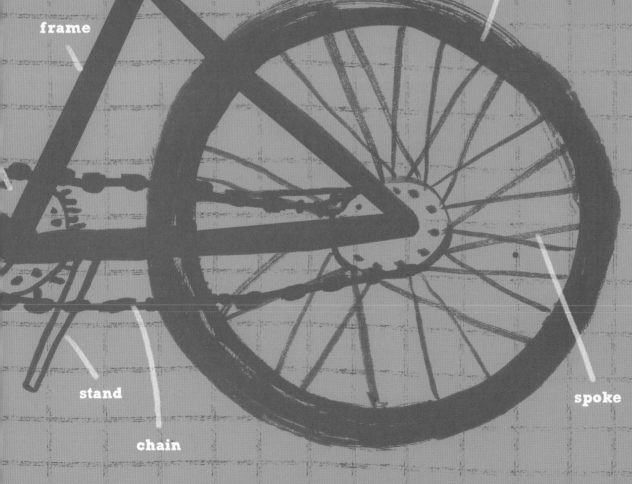

saddle

back wheel

frame

stand

chain

spoke

TOOTY FRUITY TRUCK

Orange you glad you saved that wooden clementine crate?

WHAT YOU'LL NEED

- Four 3-inch jar lids
- Light orange and dark orange paint
- Paintbrush
- 1 clementine crate
- 2 straws
- Tacky glue
- Orange paper
- Scissors
- 4 beads (with large holes)
- E-6000 glue
- 2 wooden skewers
- Hot-glue gun
- 4 feet of rope

Choose the citrus you like best for wheels—yellow lemons, green limes, or pink grapefruits!

1   Paint the outsides of the jar lids light orange and let dry. Add a second coat to cover the label, if needed.

2   Glue the straws to the bottom of the crate with tacky glue, parallel to the front edge, 2 to 3 inches from either end. Keep the crate turned over.

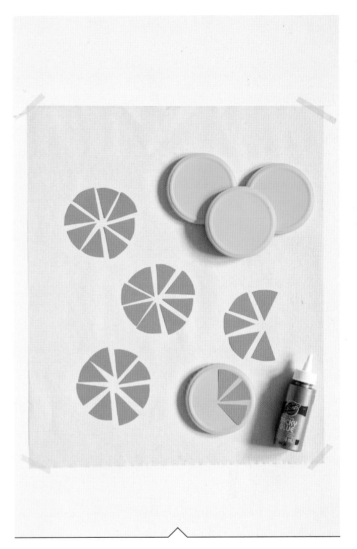

3 While the paint and glue are drying, cut four 2-inch circles from orange paper. (You can trace a roll of tape, a small bowl, or another smaller jar lid.) Cut each circle in half, then in quarters, then in eighths, to get an eight-piece pie.

4 Once the lids are dry, glue the paper wedges to the lids to create the segments of an orange (leaving a bit of space between the wedges).

5 Paint a dark orange ring around the outside of each jar lid to create the rind.

6 Using E-6000 glue, have an adult glue one bead, hole-side down, into the center of the inside of each jar lid. Let this dry completely, about 20 minutes.

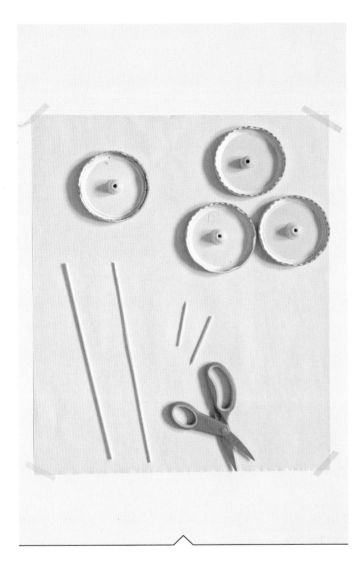

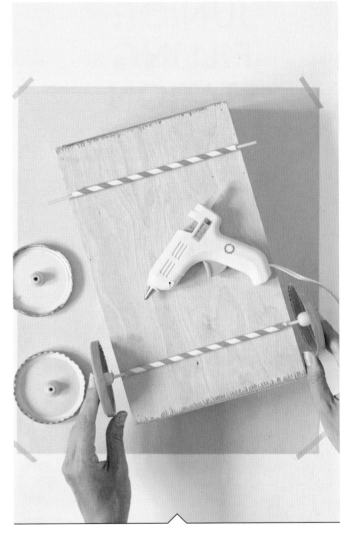

7 Trim the pointed end off of each skewer by scoring it with scissors and breaking it off, and put the skewers through the straws. You want each skewer to be about 1 inch wider than the crate.

 Have an adult squeeze a dot of hot glue into the beads glued to the center of the jar lids, then stick the lids onto the ends of each skewer. Hold the lids in place until the hot glue is set, about 2 minutes.

JUNIOR FILLING STATION

Drive your tricycle, Big Wheels, or homemade box car to the pump and fill 'er up!

WHAT YOU'LL NEED

- One 14-by-30-inch piece of ¼-inch-thick foam core

- Utility knife

- 1 adult-sized shoe box lid

- Red and white paint

- Paintbrush

- Permanent glue dots

- Red, white, and yellow scrapbook paper

- 1 clear plastic dinner plate

- Pencil

- 2- to 3-inch and ¾-inch letter stickers

- Black permanent marker

- 2 wooden skewers

- Ten ¼-inch beads

- Hot-glue gun

- Eight 1⅛-by-¾-inch spools (available from FactoryDirectCraft.com)

- Ruler

- Black pen

- Black masking tape

- ¼-inch hole punch

- 1 metal fastener

- 1 Play-Doh or tennis ball can lid

- 1 spray bottle nozzle

- 1 old jump rope

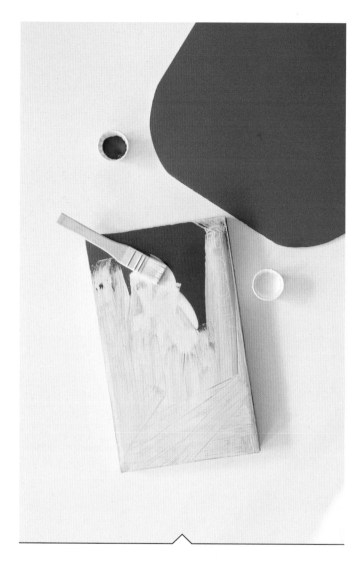

1 Have an adult round the top corners of the foam core with a utility knife. Paint one side of it red and the top of the shoe box lid white. Let both dry. Use glue dots to attach the foam core to the wall.

2 Trace and cut a circle of red paper the size of the plastic plate (minus the rim). Cut a circle of white paper about 1 inch smaller in diameter. Use glue dots to adhere the white circle on top of the red circle; spell GAS in the center of the white circle with letter stickers. Attach the paper circle to the wall with glue dots above the foam core, then use glue dots to affix the plate over the GAS sign.

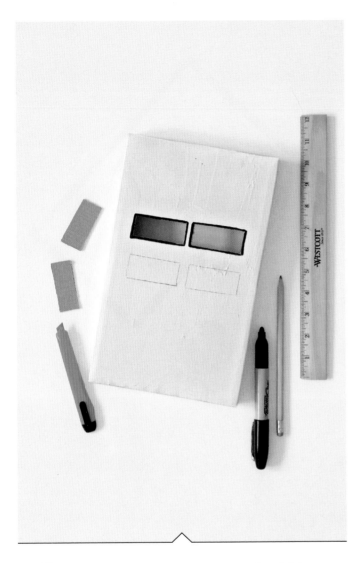

About halfway down the shoe box lid, have an adult use a utility knife to cut out four 2½-inch-wide-by-1-inch-tall windows to fit the eight spools, two per opening, with about ¼ inch between the columns and 1 inch between the rows. (If your spools are wider or longer, change the size of your windows accordingly.) Draw a black border around the edges with a permanent marker.

Slip a bead onto a skewer and have an adult hot-glue it in the center. Put two spools on either side and glue a bead 2½ inches from the center bead on either side of the spools. Repeat with the second skewer. Write three numbers around each spool.

5 Use black tape to create a border around the edge of the lid. Punch two holes on each long side of the box rim to center the skewers in the windows. Thread a skewer end through each hole, trim so just a small nub is protruding from the side of the box, and have an adult hot-glue beads to those joints. Have an adult use a utility knife to cut a ¾-inch horizontal notch about 1 inch above the top bead on the right side. (This is where the nozzle will rest.)

6 To create a clock for the pump, cut two small arrows from yellow paper, about 1 inch long. Punch holes in the ends of each arrow with a metal fastener, then push the fastener through the holes and the center of the Play-Doh lid. Use a glue dot to attach this to the shoe box lid, centered above the windows.

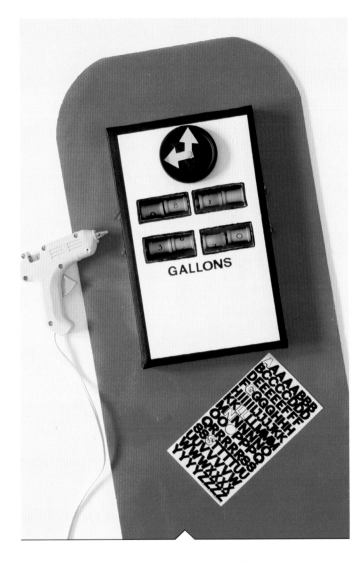

7 Have an adult hot-glue the lid to the foam core, about 4 inches down from the top. Stick the word GALLONS below the bottom row of windows and a dollar-sign sticker to the left of the top row.

8 Cut off the straw from the spray nozzle and remove the handles from the jump rope. Have an adult hot-glue one end of the jump rope just under one bottom corner of the filling station's control panel and the other end to the base of the nozzle.

ROAD TRIP!

Take your toys on a cross-country trip with the cutest handcrafted luggage you ever did see.

WHAT YOU'LL NEED

- Scissors
- Tacky glue
- Toy SUV

FOR THE SUITCASE

- New kitchen sponge (dry)
- Origami or thin craft paper
- Clear tape
- ¼-inch ribbon or leather cord

FOR THE DUFFEL BAG

- Coin roll and coin
- Brown felt
- Pen
- ¼-inch ribbon or leather cord

FOR THE SLEEPING BAG

- Thin cotton fabric
- 3 square cotton makeup-remover pads
- String

SUITCASE

Cut a rectangle from a sponge. The size of the rectangle will depend on the size of your toy vehicle, but aim for approximately a 1:16 size ratio. (For reference, our truck was 11 by 6 inches and our rectangles were about 3 by 2 inches.)

Wrap the sponge in paper (like you're wrapping a gift) and secure with tape.

Wrap a piece of leather or ribbon around the shorter dimension of the luggage, cut to size, and glue on about a quarter of the way in from the edge. Repeat for the other side. Cut a short piece of ribbon or leather and glue it on the top of the suitcase as a handle.

DUFFEL BAG

Cut a coin roll to size. (Again, judge the proportions by the size of your toy truck—our duffels were in the 2- to 3-inch range.)

Cut a piece of brown felt that wraps perfectly around the coin roll and glue in place. Now trace a coin that corresponds to the size roll that you used onto the felt and cut it out. Glue it to the end of the duffel bag. Repeat for the other end.

Wrap a piece of leather or ribbon around the circumference of the bag, cut to size, and glue on about a quarter of the way in from the edge. Repeat for the other side. Cut a short piece of ribbon or leather and glue it between the two bands as a handle.

SLEEPING BAG

 Cut a 10-by-3-inch piece of fabric.

 Now roll the fabric up, as you would a sleeping bag, and wrap with two pieces of string, knotting them to secure.

 Cut the cotton makeup-remover pads in half and lay them down the middle of the fabric strip. Fold the fabric over each side and secure with glue.

COWBOY'S COMPANION

Turn old jeans into the perfect "vehicle" on the range.

WHAT YOU'LL NEED

- Old kids' jeans, about a size 4
- Scissors
- Seam ripper (optional)
- Rubber band
- Batting
- Twine
- Brown felt
- Hot-glue gun
- 2 small black buttons
- 2 large colored buttons
- Long stick
- Bandanna

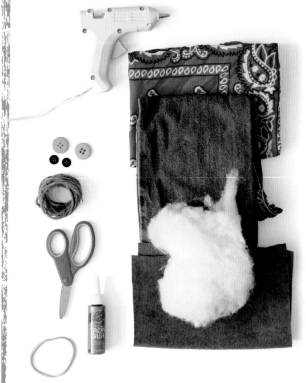

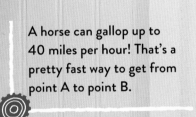

A horse can gallop up to 40 miles per hour! That's a pretty fast way to get from point A to point B.

1 Cut the jeans in half vertically, through the fly. Remove both back pockets (a seam ripper makes this a bit easier) and set aside.

2 Turn one leg inside out. Rubber band the ankle tightly, then turn the leg right-side out. Fully stuff the leg with batting.

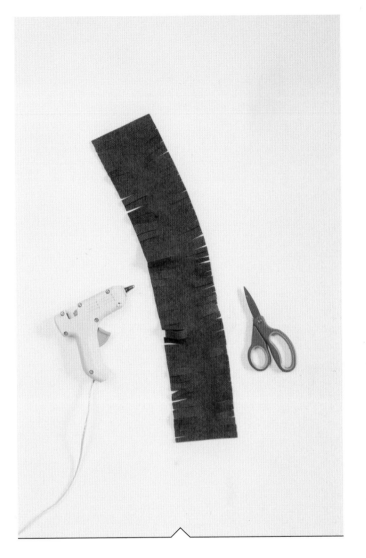

 To create the horse's head, tie the center of a 4-foot-long piece of twine around the leg about 3 inches from the rubber-banded ankle, wrapping it two or three times. Knot the twine and then bend the stuffed pant leg and wrap the twine around the thicker part of the leg (the horse's neck). Tie in a knot, leaving the remaining twine to hang off the back as reins.

 Cut a 3-inch-wide piece of brown felt, about 24 inches long. Cut a 1-inch-deep fringe along each long edge (leaving about an inch intact in the center). Have an adult apply a line of hot glue in the center and fold the felt strip in half.

 Have an adult hot-glue the edge of the fringed mane down the center of the horse's head and neck, in between the two pieces of twine.

 Have an adult hot-glue each small black button to a larger green button and hot-glue in place as eyes.

7 Fold the outside edges of each jean pocket to form an ear shape and have an adult hot-glue the ears on either side of the mane.

8 Insert a long stick into the bottom of the horse's neck and wrap tightly with the bandanna, making sure to seal in all of the batting. Giddyup!

SPARE TIRE FLOWERS

No seeds were planted in the making of these blooms!

WHAT YOU'LL NEED

- Toy wheels in various sizes
- Paint in various colors
- Paintbrush
- Felt in various colors
- Scissors
- Tacky glue
- 18-inch pieces of cloth stem wire, 20 gauge
- Thin green ribbon

1 Paint the wheels. Let dry.

2 Cut the felt into individual petal shapes. Glue them to the back of the wheels.

3 Bend a stem of wire in half and twist together. Bend the wire 90 degrees ½ inch to 1 inch from the end and glue onto the center back portion of the tire.

4 To add leaves, cut a 3-inch piece of ribbon and knot it around the stem.

BONUS PROJECT:
To make the planter, glue cotton rope all the way around a flowerpot with tacky glue. When it's dry, use a sponge brush and watercolor paint to add stripes!

TIRE-STAMPED TANK TOP

This fashionable little top would definitely be the winner on *Project Driveway*!

WHAT YOU'LL NEED

- Cotton tank top
- Towel
- 3 to 4 rubber toy wheels in various sizes
- VersaCraft ink pads in various colors
- Stamp cleaner
- Iron

1 Lay a towel underneath the tank top. This allows for some give when you press your stamp onto the fabric.

2 Dab a rubber tire onto an ink pad to collect a generous amount of ink and press it onto the fabric.

3 Repeat step 2 with various colors and wheels, making sure to clean the tires with stamp cleaner before switching colors.

4 Iron the tank top to set the ink into the fabric before washing.

Rubber toy tires work much better for this project than hard plastic. Their sponginess resembles a classic rubber stamp.

FUSIBLE-BEAD BICYCLE

Ambling through the countryside on two wheels is the perfect way to take in your surroundings!

WHAT YOU'LL NEED

- Black and teal fusible plastic beads (available from Michaels.com)
- 3-inch round Perler bead form
- Parchment paper
- Iron
- Bicycle template (download at ProjectKid.com/bike)
- Computer, printer, and printer paper
- One 10-by-12-inch piece of cardboard
- Tape
- 10 straight pins
- Red yarn
- Scissors
- Tacky glue
- Paintbrush

Fusible plastic beads were invented more than fifty years ago by a company that made plastic drinking straws!

To make the bike's **tires**, place black beads all around the outer ring of the bead form. Add **spokes** by creating a six-point asterisk with the teal beads, leaving the center hole empty.

Following the instructions on the bead packaging, have an adult fuse the beads together using parchment paper and an iron; let cool completely. Repeat steps 1 and 2 to make a second tire. Remove the fused beads from the form.

 Download and print the bike template and place on the cardboard. Tape parchment paper over it.

4 Insert straight pins as vertically as you can into the ten marked points on the template.

5 Thread yarn through the center hole of one wheel, and begin wrapping the yarn around the pins to create the bike form, following the numbers on the template.

6 Work your way over to the second wheel and thread the yarn through. Continue wrapping around the pins, following the numbers on the template.

7 Once the full bicycle frame is completed, knot the yarn and trim the end.

8 Use a paintbrush to apply a generous coat of tacky glue to the yarn, and let it dry. Remove the pins and flip over to apply an additional coat of glue to the back of the yarn if needed.

MODERN MOBILE HOME

Glue this minimalist house to its trailer or leave it separate so you can play with it in other ways—making it truly mobile!

WHAT YOU'LL NEED

- One 10-by-13-inch piece of cardboard
- Pencil
- Scissors
- 2 pieces of balsa wood: one 36 by 3 by $\frac{3}{16}$ inch, one 6 by 12½ inches
- Utility knife
- Sandpaper
- Hot-glue gun
- Patterned craft paper
- Glue stick
- Green felt
- Tacky glue
- 4 toy cars of like size
- String
- Toy truck

FOR THE HOME DECORATIONS (OPTIONAL)

- Paper party hat
- Black masking tape
- Large round bead or small Styrofoam ball
- Black thread
- Furniture and window frame templates (download at ProjectKid.com/mobilehome)
- Computer, printer, and printer paper
- Card stock
- Black permanent marker
- 3-by-2-inch photo of countryside

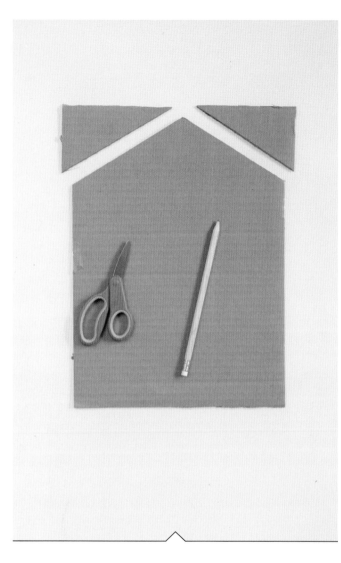

1   With the cardboard rectangle resting vertically on your work surface, make a mark 3 inches from the top on each side of the rectangle and one mark at the halfway point at the top of the rectangle. Draw two straight lines connecting these marks to create a house shape and cut. Set aside.

2   Have an adult use a utility knife to cut the large piece of balsa wood into five 3-inch-wide pieces: two 6¼-inch, two 10-inch, and one 10¼-inch.

3 Holding the sandpaper with one hand flat on your work surface, sand one edge of each of the short pieces to a 45-degree angle. (Balsa wood is very soft and easy for kids to work with.) Do the same thing with the two 10-inch pieces. Once the child is finished, an adult may want to go back and adjust the angles so that the joints fit together well.

4 Have an adult hot-glue the joints together, matching up the 45-degree angles on the short pieces at the peak of the roof and the 45-degree angles on the long pieces under the eaves. Add the floor by gluing the 10¼-inch piece to the bottom edges of the two side pieces.

5 Trace the cardboard shape onto patterned craft paper; since the dimensions of the cardboard and paper don't quite match, you'll need two separate sections of the paper. First, align the cardboard shape flush to the top and left edges of the paper, trace, and cut out. You'll be left with a strip of paper you can trace, cut out, and use to cover the bottom portion of the cardboard shape.

6 To make the trailer for the mobile home, trace your 6-by-12½-inch piece of balsa wood onto the green felt. Cut out the felt shape and glue it to the wood with tacky glue. Flip the trailer over and have an adult hot-glue a toy car to each corner (with the cars facing the sides of the house). Glue a piece of string to the bottom of the trailer and tie to the back of a toy truck.

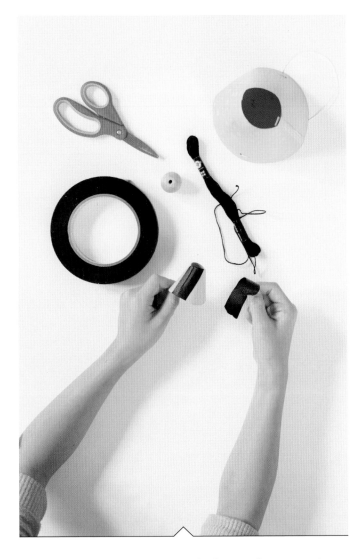

 If you want to give the home a lamp, cut about 1½ inches off the top of a party hat, and then cut off about ¼ inch from the point so that it's open on both sides. Cover in black tape. Put a bead or Styrofoam ball inside the shade so it acts as a stopper. Thread a string up through the bead (or around the ball) with 5 inches of black thread. Have an adult hot-glue the end of the string to the ceiling of the house, about 3 inches from the corner.

 If you wish, download and print furniture templates (or photos of furniture from the Internet) and the window frame template onto card stock. If using photos, color them black and cut them out. Print a 3-by-2-inch photo from a recent drive through the countryside and glue the window frame over it. Use a glue stick to adhere the furniture and window to the wall of your house.

WATER

⚓

Hello, Sailor!	Beach Time
Night Light-House	Sponge Tugboat
Aquatic Flag Garland	Ship of Foods
Coast Guard Life Jacket	Yellow Submarine
Underwater Puppet Theater	

Parts of
a **SAILBOAT**,
SUBMARINE, and
LIGHTHOUSE

SAILBOAT

mast

mainsail

jib

boom

hull

rudder

propeller

SUBMARINE

porthole

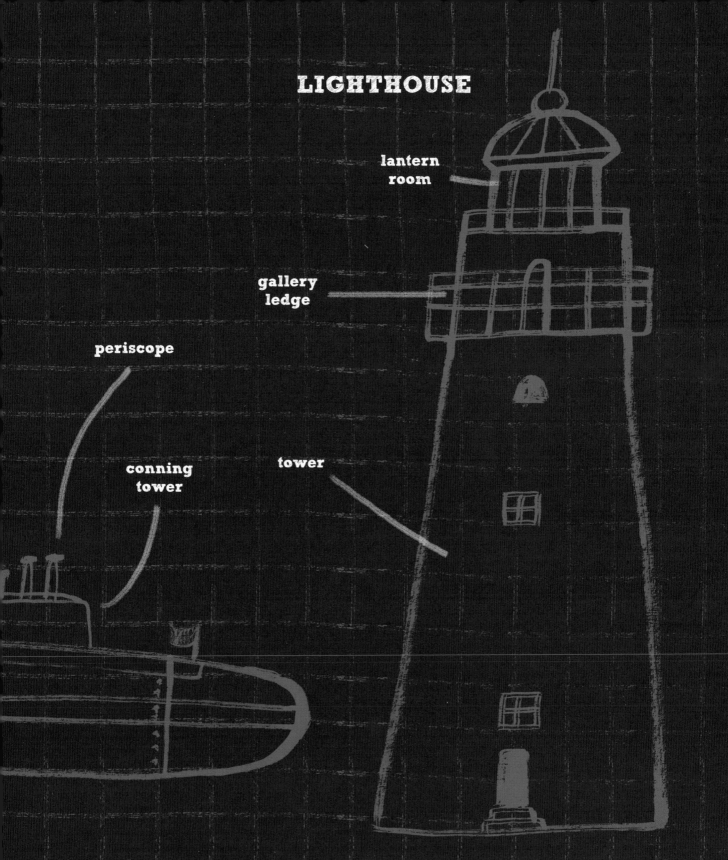

LIGHTHOUSE

lantern
room

gallery
ledge

periscope

conning
tower

tower

HELLO, SAILOR!

After a fresh batch of laundry is fluffed and folded, take your basket to the high seas.

- One 40-inch stick or dowel
- One 18-inch stick or dowel
- Thin cotton rope
- One 24-by-18-inch piece of fabric or bedsheet
- Scissors
- Hot-glue gun (optional)
- Fabric scraps
- 1 laundry basket

1 To make the **mast** and the **boom**, cross the short stick perpendicularly over the long stick about 24 inches down from one end and wrap the joint, making figure eights back and forth around the sticks, with about 2 feet of cotton rope.

2 To make the **sail**, cut your piece of fabric in half diagonally. Place the right corner of the sail where the mast and the boom meet. For a quick assembly, have an adult hot-glue the fabric edges to the mast and the boom, or tie your sail on: Use your scissors to poke holes about every 3 inches along the two perpendicular edges of the fabric, about 1 inch in from the edge. Cut 4-inch pieces of rope and thread them through the holes and around the sticks.

3 Cut an 80-inch piece of rope and tie strips of fabric scraps you might have every 3 to 5 inches along the rope. Tie the rope to the top of the mast, and let it hang down.

4 Use rope to tie the mast to the side of the basket, securing it through the holes in at least two places.

NIGHT LIGHT-HOUSE

Vegetable oil, dish soap, organic juice: your home is full of products in unusually shaped bottles that can be transformed into this perfect shoreline structure.

WHAT YOU'LL NEED

- One 10-ounce plastic bottle, empty and dry (mine was a Method Home hand-soap bottle)
- 1 black tennis ball can lid
- Black permanent marker
- Scissors
- Red and white sand (available from Michaels.com)
- Funnel
- Black electrical tape
- One 4-ounce baby food jar
- 1 battery-powered votive
- Permanent glue dots (optional)

The sand makes this project sturdy enough to double as a bookend.

Martin / Carle   Brown Bear, Brown Bear, What Do You See?   Henry Holt

Barton   Trains

Barton   Planes

Barton   Boats

CD TO A PARTY!   HYPERION DBG

1

To create the lighthouse's **gallery ledge**, center the opening of the empty bottle on the tennis ball can lid and trace. Cut a slit into the plastic and cut out the circle. Set this aside.

2

Use the funnel to pour alternating layers of red and white sand into the bottle. (You can measure out even stripes or just eyeball it.) To level out each layer of sand, tap the bottle on your work surface a few times. Fill all the way to the top and seal the opening with electrical tape.

 Wrap electrical tape around the threaded part of the baby food jar, and color the bottom of the outside of the jar with black permanent marker. Slip the gallery ledge around the mouth of the bottle.

4 To create the lighthouse's **lantern room**, stand the battery-powered votive on top of the bottle and cover it with the baby food jar. (My jar lid sat perfectly atop the bottle and votive, but if you find yours is less steady, use glue dots to keep it in place.)

AQUATIC FLAG GARLAND

Rickrack, the sassy sister of ribbon, is obviously the perfect ready-made material to create waves for this sun print garland.

WHAT YOU'LL NEED

- ¼-inch- and ½-inch-wide rickrack

- Scissors

- Large shallow bowl

- Sun print paper (available from MagicCabin.com)

- Tray or oversized book

- Glass or plexi sheet (optional)

- Paper towels

- Anchor template (download at ProjectKid.com/anchor)

- Computer, printer, and printer paper

- Light blue card stock

- Glue stick

- ¼-inch hole punch

- String

Cut rickrack into 6-inch pieces, about five of each size, and fill your bowl with water.

 Pull out a piece of sun print paper, lay it on a tray, and quickly arrange the rickrack strips horizontally on the paper.

 Download the anchor template on card stock, print, and cut out.

 Use the anchor to make sun prints following the procedure in steps 2 and 3.

Take the paper into the bright sunlight and let it sit until it turns a light blue, about 2 minutes. (If it's a windy day, use a piece of glass or plexi from a picture frame to hold the rickrack strips in place.)

 When the paper is ready, take it inside and soak it in the water bath for a minute, and then lay it out to dry on a paper towel. Repeat for as many prints as you'd like to make.

 To turn your prints into flags, cut a 2-inch-tall triangle out of the bottom of each sun print, then mount the print onto card stock with a glue stick. Trim around the flag, leaving about a ¼-inch border of card stock on all sides.

 Punch holes in the top corners of each flag and thread string through to complete the garland.

COAST GUARD LIFE JACKET

Don this vest while patrolling the waters, shoreline, or just your backyard kiddie pool.

WHAT YOU'LL NEED

- 1 paper grocery bag
- Pencil
- Scissors
- Large bubble wrap
- Orange and silver duct tape
- Black 1-inch letter stickers
- Computer, printer, and 2-inch-diameter circle labels (optional)

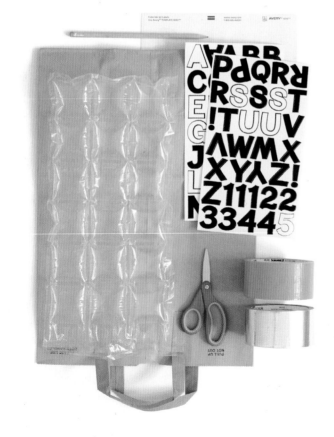

While this paper-bag life preserver looks totally authentic, do not attempt to use it as a flotation device.

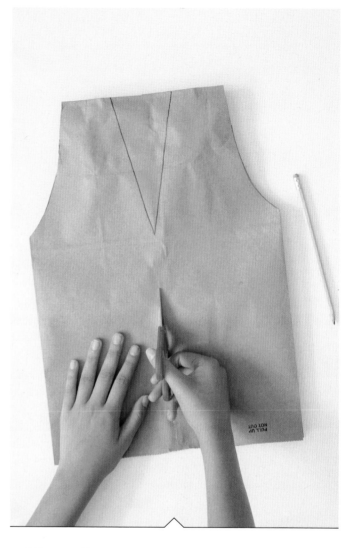

With your paper grocery bag lying flat with the open edge closest to you, draw armholes in pencil on either side of the bag, starting about 2 inches in from the top corners and swooping down to just above the crease that creates the bottom of the bag. (Open the bag and check out the armholes. Cut off any excess flaps to create a clean opening.)

To make the head hole, draw a V shape from the top down to the crease in the bag that creates the bottom. Make sure the V shape is narrow enough to leave the vest's straps at least 2 inches wide. Cut straight up the middle of one side of the bag, and then cut out the V shape; continue to cut straight to the back of the bag's bottom. Cut this piece out to create the head hole.

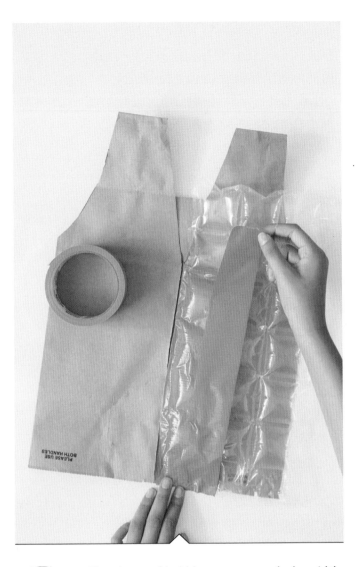

U.S.
COAST
GUA

3 Cut pieces of bubble wrap to match the width of each half of the front of the vest. Lay the bubble wrap on each of the front panels and cover them with orange tape, wrapping the edges of the tape around to the underside of the jacket. Continue covering the vest with tape until the entire thing is orange.

4 Add a diagonal strip of silver tape to each front panel as shown on page 149. With letter stickers, write U.S. COAST GUARD on the back of the vest. If you wish, you can download the U.S. Coast Guard symbol from the Internet, print it onto a 2-inch round label, and adhere it to the front of the vest.

UNDERWATER PUPPET THEATER

Put on a dramatic shadow puppet show for friends and family, complete with fish, sharks, and submarines.

WHAT YOU'LL NEED

- One 16-by-20-inch white frame with mat (mine was a Ribba frame from IKEA)
- Blue and white acrylic paint
- Paintbrush
- Vellum
- Scissors
- Clear tape
- Hot-glue gun
- Blue poster board
- Permanent glue dots
- Seaweed, fish, shark, and submarine templates (download at ProjectKid.com/underwater)
- Computer, printer, and printer paper
- Green and black card stock
- Pencil
- 6-inch-by-6-inch patterned origami paper
- Wooden skewers
- 1 small gooseneck desk lamp

Remove the glass, backing, and mat from the frame and discard the glass and backing (or save for another project). Paint the front of the mat blue and the inside of the frame white.

 Cut vellum to fit over the opening of the mat and tape it on the unpainted side of the mat. Have an adult hot-glue the mat into the frame with the blue side facing the original back of the frame.

Fold an origami boat (see pages 156–157 for the how-to) and affix it with glue dots to the top of the frame, behind the wave strip.

Download and print fish, shark, and submarine templates and trace onto black card stock. Cut out the underwater shapes and attach to skewers with clear tape.

Cut a 3-inch-wide and 20-inch-long piece of blue poster board. Cut one long edge to look like a wave. Attach the wave strip to the top front edge of the frame with glue dots.

 Download and print the seaweed templates and trace onto green card stock (or draw your own, making sure to add a 1-inch-square tab on the bottom). Cut out the shapes, fold back the tabs, and use glue dots to adhere to the bottom, inside edge of the frame.

 Position the lamp 2 to 3 feet behind the theater, shining directly onto the vellum.

 Lights, camera . . . action!

ORIGAMI BOAT

1 The side of your paper that is faceup on your work surface will be the hull, not the sails. Make a diagonal crease by folding one corner to the opposite corner and unfold.

2 Repeat with the other two corners and unfold.

3 Turn the paper over and fold it in half, creating a rectangle. Then unfold.

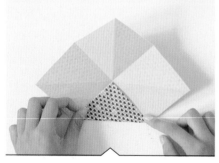

7 Unfold the square slightly and fold the bottom front corner inside to the very center.

8 Turn it over and repeat on the other side.

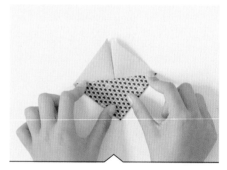

9 Push the sides back in to return it to a diamond shape. This time, the diamond will have two separate triangles (in this case, peach) on top (the **sails**) and a larger triangle on the bottom (the **hull**).

4 Turn the paper 90 degrees and fold it in half again, leaving it folded. The folded edge should be along the bottom with creases that form a V shape.

5 Pinch the folded edge of the paper on either side of the V shape and bring your fingers together, so that the four corners all come together at the top. Fold into a square shape.

6 Place the now small square flat on the work surface in a diamond position. There should be two flaps to the right and two flaps to the left of the center vertical crease.

10 Fold the right sail triangle down over the hull, so the top point of the sail meets the bottom point of the hull.

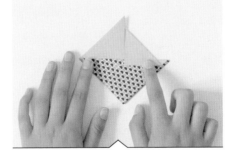

11 Fold the right triangle back up at a point slightly below the level of the hull; this "sail" should now be smaller than the other "sail." Tuck the pleat at the bottom of the sail between the layers of the hull.

12 Fold the bottom corner of the hull up to the top edge of the hull, where the two sails meet, then unfold it slightly to make a "stand" for the boat.

BEACH TIME

Make some waves with this simple clock craft.

WHAT YOU'LL NEED

- One 10-inch round wooden clock surface (available from Michaels.com)

- Pencil

- Scrapbook paper: 1 yellow and 3 blue patterns

- Scissors

- Extra-strength glue stick

- ¾-inch rope

- Adhesive white felt (available from Michaels.com)

- Permanent glue dots with dispenser

- 1 cereal or cracker box

- Paddle clock hands templates (download at ProjectKid.com/clock)

- Computer, printer, and printer paper

- ⅛-inch hole punch

- One ¾-inch quartz clock movement kit (available from Michaels.com)

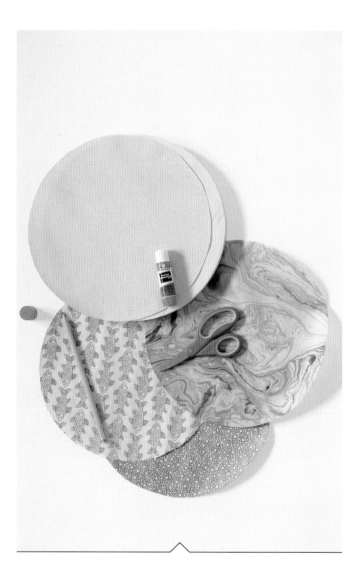

1 Trace the clock surface onto the yellow and blue papers and cut out the circles. Rub the clock surface with a generous coating of glue stick and position the yellow circle on top. Smooth out the paper to remove any bubbles.

2 Cut one blue circle in half, and then cut a jagged wave pattern across the cut edge. Coat the back of the paper with the glue stick and position on the clock face. Repeat for the next two blue papers, cutting them each about 1 inch shorter than the preceding paper.

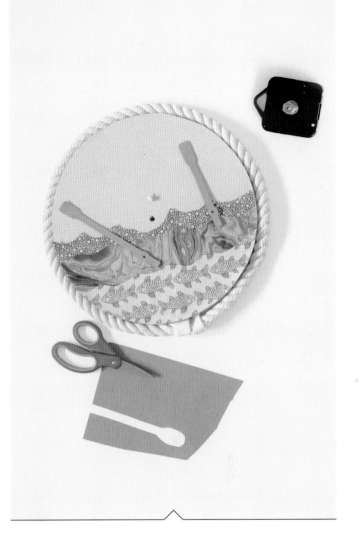

3   Cut a 32-inch length of rope and two small tabs of adhesive felt. Wrap the felt around the ends of the rope to prevent fraying. Apply a generous amount of glue dots along the side edge of the clock, and then wrap the rope around it, pressing firmly so that the dots grab hold of both the wood and the rope.

4   Unfold the cracker or cereal box. Download and print the paddle templates and trace them onto the brown side of the box. Cut them out. Punch a hole at the end of each paddle and use them as the clock hands. Attach the clock movement kit according to the package instructions.

SPONGE TUGBOAT

When this seafaring vessel fills up with water, just wring her out and set her on her merry way.

WHAT YOU'LL NEED

- Seven 3-by-5-inch scrubber sponges
- One 5-by-7-inch mesh scrubber sponge
- Fabric glue
- Scissors
- Five 3-by-5-inch sponges
- Binder clip
- 1 sponge cloth
- 1-inch circle punch
- Black craft foam
- String
- 1 old towel with a hem
- 1 wooden skewer

The tires on the sides of a tugboat protect it when it bumps into other tugboats. Maybe they should be called bumper boats!

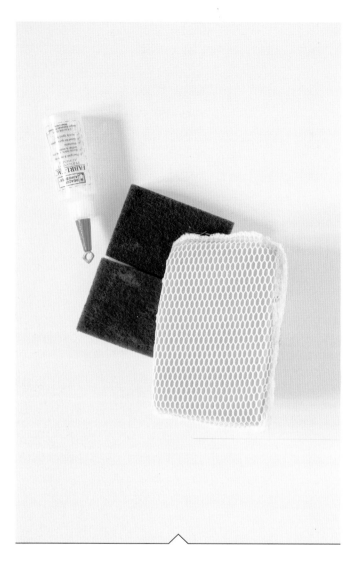

 1 Lay two scrubber sponges long end to long end and glue the mesh scrubber on top so that it completely covers them.

2 Cut two regular 3-by-5-inch sponges in half lengthwise and glue them around the outer edge of the scrubber base, gluing the front two segments together into a point. Use a binder clip to hold in place.

Cut a 1-by-5-inch strip from a regular 3-by-5-inch sponge and glue it across the back of the boat. Cut one edge of the strip into a wavy shape.

To make the boat's cabin, lay two 3-by-5-inch scrubber sponges side by side, stack two more scrubber sponges on top of them, and glue all four together. Stack two regular 3-by-5-inch sponges on top of this block and glue them together and to the scrubbers. Top it off with one more 3-by-5-inch scrubber sponge and glue.

5 To make the portholes, punch eight circles from the dry sponge cloth and glue four on each side of the boat.

6 To make tires, cut out four to six circles from craft foam about 2 inches in diameter; using the circle punch or scissors, cut a 1-inch hole in the center of each to give it a tire shape.

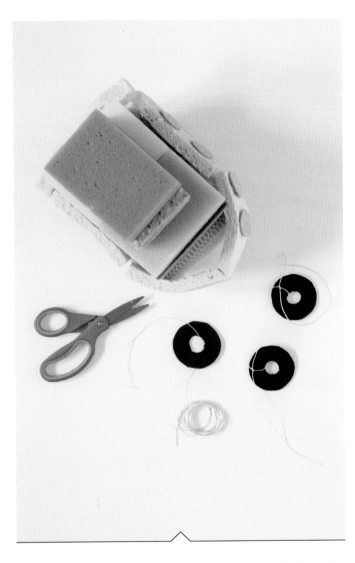

7 Tie a 5-inch piece of string onto each tire and glue the other ends of the strings in between the sponges on the deck on both sides of the boat.

8 To make a flag for the boat, cut a 3-by-4-inch rectangle from the edge of the towel (the 3-inch side should include the towel's corner, with the hem). Insert the skewer through the hem and drive the pointy end down into the sponge boat. Secure with glue at both ends if needed.

SHIP OF FOODS

A boat made out of chopsticks, a bread loaf pan, and a slice of pizza just can't go by any other name.

WHAT YOU'LL NEED

- 4 felt squares: 9-inch khaki, 6-inch yellow, 2-inch green, and 5-inch red

- Pencil

- Scissors

- Tacky glue

- Fringe scissors (optional)

- Fabric Mod Podge

- Foam brush

- Hot-glue gun

- One 1-inch spool

- One 4½-by-2½-inch rectangular cardboard loaf pan (available from WelcomeHomeBrands.com)

- 2 chopsticks

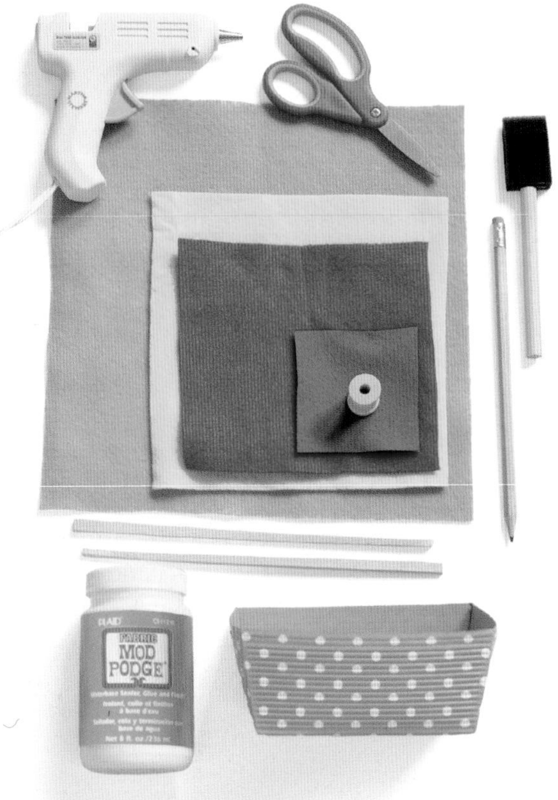

To make the pizza sail, draw a line from the center point of the top edge of the khaki felt square down to each bottom corner of the square, creating a triangle. Cut along those lines and discard the two smaller triangles. To make the pizza crust, fold the bottom edge of the triangle up about an inch and glue it in place. Trim the corners to create a clean edge.

To make the pizza cheese, cut narrow parallel strips about 1 inch long into the yellow felt square (or use fringe scissors). Once you've finished fringing one side of the felt square, cut off these strips. Continue fringing and cutting the felt until you have enough "cheese" to cover the surface of the pizza. Cut 1-inch pepperoni circles from the red felt and little green pepper half-moons from the green felt as toppings.

3   Coat the pizza with Mod Podge and press the yellow felt slivers onto the triangular slice. Then use Mod Podge to stick the pepperoni and peppers on top. Let dry for at least 20 minutes.

4   Have an adult hot-glue the spool to the bottom center of the loaf pan (the **hull**). Then hot-glue two chopsticks together to create a 12-inch-tall **mast**. Hot-glue the mast down the center of the pizza sail, and then into the hole of the spool.

YELLOW SUBMARINE

Kids will have a ball with this submarine bath toy.

WHAT YOU'LL NEED

- 3 bottle caps
- Green acrylic paint
- Paintbrush
- 1 used pod from a single-cup coffeemaker, cleaned out
- Yellow electrical tape
- 1 flexible straw
- Scissors
- Foam football
- E-6000 glue
- Cap from GoGo Squeez applesauce

1 Paint the bottle caps green.

2 While the paint is drying, wrap the sides of the coffee pod in tape.

3 To create the sub's **periscope**, cut the straw about 3½ inches from the flexible section, and push down into the hole at the bottom of the coffee pod. (The coffeemakers punch a hole when the hot water filters through the coffee grounds.)

4 Using E-6000 glue, have an adult glue the bottle caps onto the side of the foam football as **portholes**, the pod onto the top as the **conning tower**, and the applesauce cap onto the back point to create the **propeller**. Let the glue dry for at least 12 hours before taking the sub on its first underwater bathtub voyage.

DIRT

Custom Construction Vehicle

Tire Tread Stamp

Big Dig Terrarium

Felt Safety Signs

DIY Erector Sets

Parts of
CONSTRUCTION VEHICLES

CRANE TRUCK

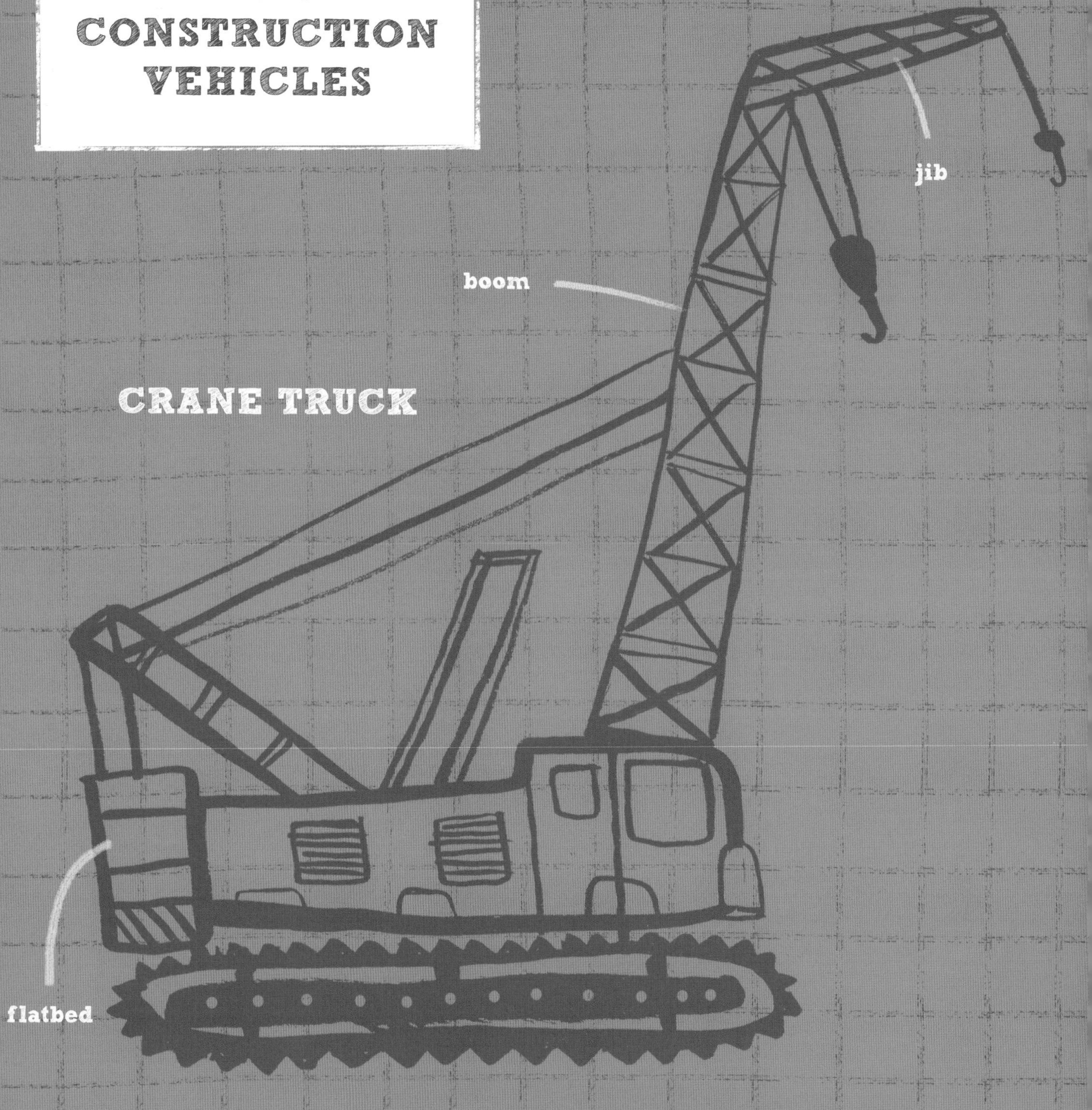
jib
boom
flatbed

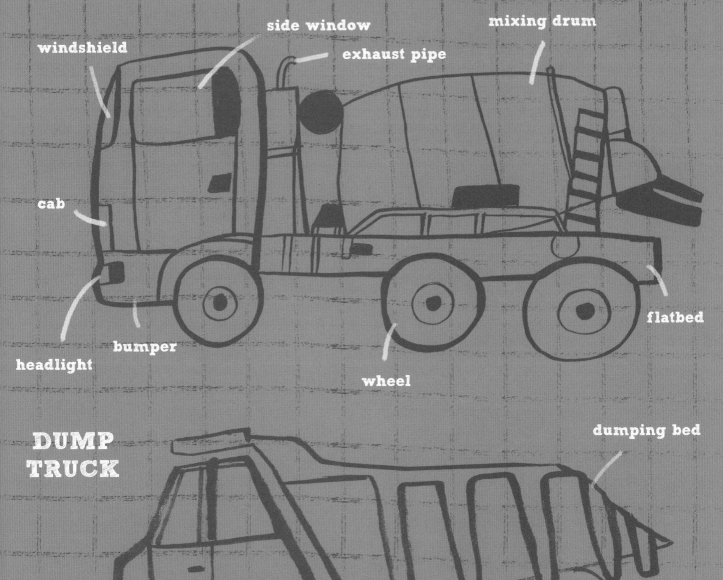

CEMENT TRUCK

windshield

side window

exhaust pipe

mixing drum

cab

headlight

bumper

wheel

flatbed

DUMP TRUCK

dumping bed

flatbed

CUSTOM CONSTRUCTION VEHICLE

Build the same base for each truck, then turn to pages 184–185 to outfit your vehicle of choice.

turn to pages 184–185

- 1 child-sized shoe box lid
- Duct tape: colored (to match your choice of truck, below) and silver
- Black paper
- Scissors
- Tacky glue
- One ¼-inch balsa-wood dowel
- 6 metal washers: four 1½-inch and two ½-inch
- Four 1-inch plastic washers
- One 2-inch-thick piece of Styrofoam
- Plastic knife
- Wide smoothie straw

FOR THE DUMP TRUCK

- Plastic butter container
- Green duct tape

FOR THE CEMENT TRUCK

- One 1-by-1-by-1-inch block of Styrofoam
- Yellow duct tape
- Tacky glue
- Adhesive Velcro
- Lemon saver (available from BedBathandBeyond.com)

FOR THE CRANE TRUCK

- One 1-by-2-inch piece of Styrofoam, the width of your shoe box
- Blue duct tape
- 3 blue tongue depressors
- ⅛-inch hole punch
- 2 yellow metal fasteners

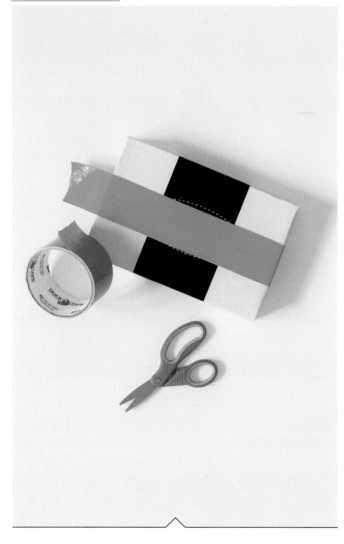

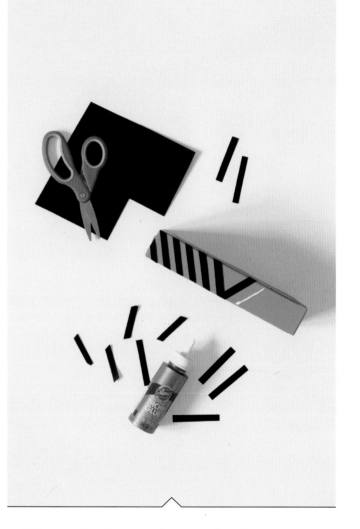

 To create the truck's **flatbed**, cover the shoe box lid in colored duct tape.

Cut ¼-inch-wide strips of black paper and glue them about ¼ inch apart along each long side of the lid, half running diagonally from the right and half diagonally from the left. To create the truck's **bumpers**, cut four ¼-inch-wide-by-2-inch-long strips and glue two to the front and two to the back sides of the lid.

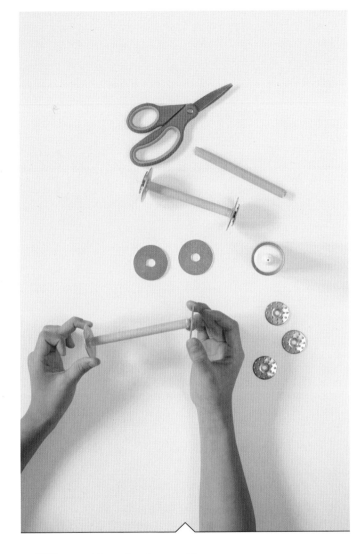

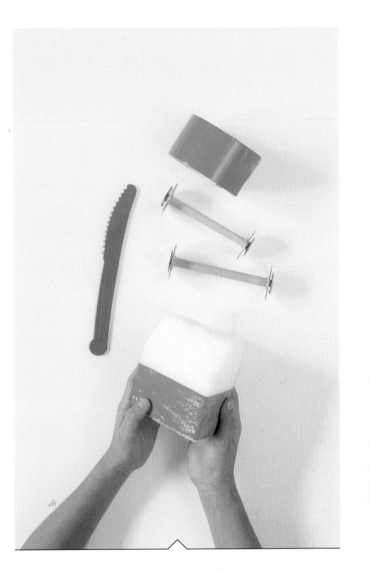

 To make the truck's **wheel axles**, score two dowels with scissors and break to about ½ inch wider than your box lid. To add the **wheels**, twist a 1½-inch metal washer onto both ends of each dowel, and then glue the plastic washers on top.

 While the wheel glue is drying, make the truck's **cab** by cutting the Styrofoam with a plastic knife into a rectangle that is 4 inches tall and the width of your box lid. Slice off one corner diagonally to create the surface for the windshield. Cover the Styrofoam in colored duct tape.

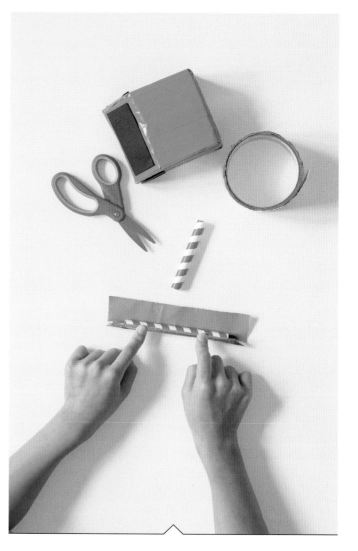

5 Cut a rectangle from black paper about 1 inch shorter than the width of the cab as the **windshield**, and two 1-inch right triangles for the **side windows** and cut off the top points. Glue onto the Styrofoam with tacky glue.

6 To make the truck's **exhaust pipe**, cut the straw so that it's about ½ inch taller than the Styrofoam block. Tear a piece of silver duct tape that's a bit longer than the straw and roll the straw in the tape. Push the excess into either end of the straw.

7 To attach the wheel axles, turn the box top over. Tear two 4-inch pieces of duct tape and fold in half lengthwise to create 4-by-1-inch strips. Lay the dowels across the edges of the lid, about 1 inch from either end. Adhere the duct-tape strips over the dowels to the underside of the box with small pieces of duct tape.

8 To make the **headlights**, glue the ½-inch metal washers to the bottom corners of the truck's cab. Glue the cab onto the front of the box top and glue the exhaust pipe against the back of the cab.

DUMP TRUCK

To create the **dumping bed**, cover the outside of the butter container in duct tape.

2 Line up the edge of the dumping bed with the back edge of the flatbed and attach it down the back with a vertical piece of colored duct tape. Tilt the dumping bed back and adhere another piece of tape underneath, sealing the hinge and securing it to the flatbed.

CEMENT TRUCK

Using a plastic knife, cut the 1-inch-square piece of Styrofoam in half diagonally. Cover it with yellow duct tape.

Glue the wedge to the flatbed of the truck with the angled edge pointing toward the back of the truck.

To make the **mixing drum**, adhere Velcro to the angled edge of the Styrofoam wedge and to the bottom of the lemon saver. Attach the lemon saver to the Styrofoam triangle.

CRANE TRUCK

 Cover the piece of Styrofoam in blue duct tape and glue this piece to the back edge of the flatbed.

 Use the blade of a pair of scissors to cut a small slit toward the cab in the middle of this new piece of Styrofoam.

 To create the crane's **boom** and **jib**, have an adult punch holes in one end of two tongue depressors, and both ends of one depressor.

 Attach the pieces of the crane together with metal fasteners. Insert one end of the boom into the slit and move into the desired position.

TIRE TREAD STAMP

Use these track stamps to decorate just about anything! And experiment with different tire tread shapes to create your own patterns.

WHAT YOU'LL NEED

- Craft foam
- Scissors
- Cardboard
- Tacky glue
- Black ink pad
- Item you wish to stamp (such as a cork place mat, a wooden pencil box, a brown lunch bag, or a notepad)

1 Cut six ½-by-1-inch rectangles from craft foam.

2 Glue two rectangles to a small piece of cardboard in a V shape, lining up one short end with the end of a long side. Repeat two more times to create a three-tread stamp. Let the glue dry.

3 Cut the cardboard close around the top and bottom edges of the V shape. (This will help you stamp precisely to create an even track.)

4 Ink up the stamp by tapping numerous times on an ink pad and pressing evenly onto your chosen surface.

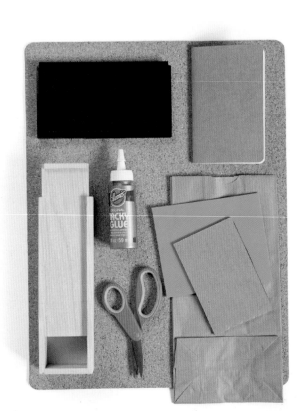

BIG DIG TERRARIUM

Like construction sites, terrariums are a work in progress, always changing and growing. And also full of dirt.

WHAT YOU'LL NEED

FOR THE CONSTRUCTION BARRICADE

- 1 tongue depressor
- 2 Popsicle sticks
- 1 thin Popsicle stick
- White and orange paint
- Paintbrush
- White pipe cleaner
- Scissors

FOR THE TERRARIUM

- 1 wide glass container with lid
- Pea gravel
- Activating charcoal
- Soil
- Small construction vehicles (available from MagicCabin.com)
- Plants

Plants in a closed terrarium survive on the humidity that is created in this airtight environment. Good small plants for terrariums are moss, angel's tears, silver nerve plants, and miniature ferns. You want to make sure that all of your plants have the same watering needs!

CONSTRUCTION BARRICADE

 Paint one side of the tongue depressor and all three Popsicle sticks white and let them dry. Repeat on the other side. Paint orange diagonal stripes across the tongue depressor. Let dry.

 Cut the tongue depressor into two 2-inch pieces and cut the Popsicle sticks in half. Cut the rounded ends off both of the thin Popsicle stick pieces.

 Glue two of the wider Popsicle stick halves to the back of each painted tongue depressor piece to create the legs of the barricade. Glue the thin Popsicle stick sections across the middle of the legs, forming an H shape. Let the glue dry.

 Cut the pipe cleaner to match the width of the barricade. Glue this piece of pipe cleaner in between the two sides of the barricade at the top. Separate the legs to form an upside-down V shape.

TERRARIUM

 Fill the bottom of a glass container with about 1 inch of pea gravel. Pour about 1 inch of charcoal on top of the gravel. Top with about 2 inches of soil.

 Place the construction vehicles and barricade in the terrarium, along with some plants or seeds (see tip on page 189). Replace the lid.

FELT SAFETY SIGNS

Send a clear message to all passersby with these eye-catching stenciled banners.

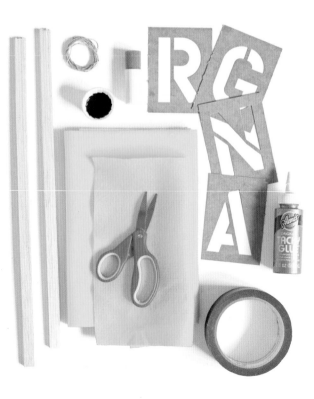

1 Cut a piece of felt into a rectangle. (For KIDS @ WORK, cut a 15-by-12-inch rectangle; for CAUTION, cut a 10-by-12-inch rectangle; for DETOUR, cut a 12-by-12-inch rectangle.) To create the point at the bottom of the sign, fold the rectangle in half and cut from the bottom of the center fold, diagonally, to about 2 inches above the two stacked open corners.

2 Arrange your chosen letter/symbol stencils on the banner, tape them together, then tape them to the felt.

3 Dab small amounts of paint into the letters using the stencil brush. Be careful—if you use too much paint, it will seep underneath the stencil edges. Remove the stencils immediately after painting and let the banners dry.

4 Trim the dowels to measure about 2 inches wider than the banner. Cut a 20- to 24-inch-long piece of string. Glue one dowel to the back top edge of the banner, lay one end of the string on either corner, then glue the other dowel onto the front top edge of the banner (sandwiching the string in between the two dowels). Let dry before hanging.

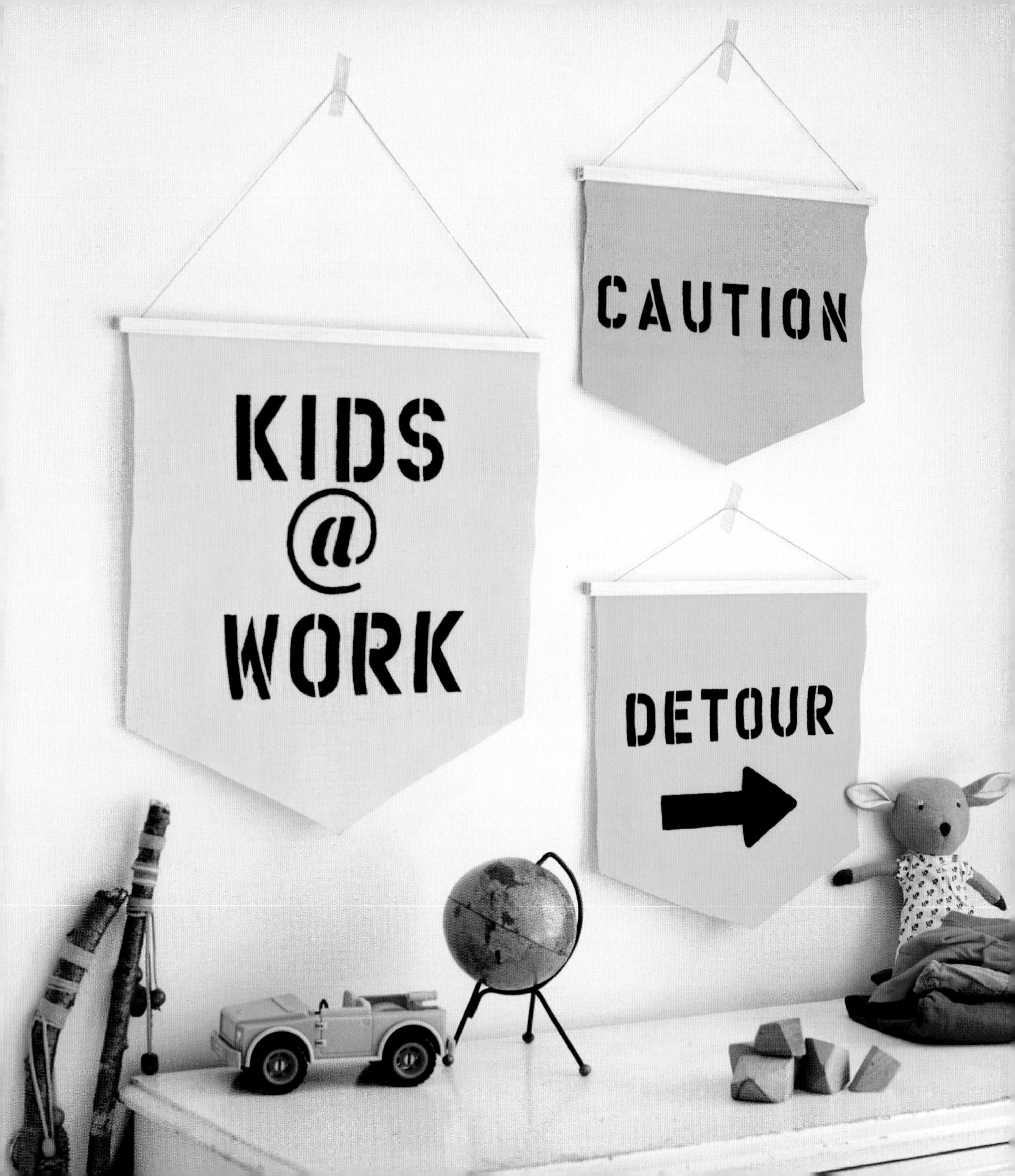
KIDS
@
WORK
CAUTION
DETOUR

DIY ERECTOR SETS

You don't need expensive Legos or Erector sets to build tall structures. These three projects all require just a few simple materials.

WHAT YOU'LL NEED

FOR THE STRAW STRUCTURES

- Pipe cleaners
- Scissors
- Straws

FOR THE CLAY CONSTRUCTION

- Model Magic clay
- Toothpicks

FOR THE CARDBOARD CREATIONS

- Cardboard
- Scissors
- Pencil
- Colored duct tape

STRAW STRUCTURES

1 Cut the pipe cleaners into four equal pieces.

2 Insert pipe cleaners into straws to connect and build. To create corners, bend pipe cleaner segments into right angles. To make a longer straw, connect two straws with a straight piece of pipe cleaner.

3 To create a roof, bend four pieces of pipe cleaner about 45 degrees. Insert into the top corners of the structure, pointing inward, and add four new straws so they meet in the middle. Connect at the roof's peak with two pipe cleaner segments, crossed over one another and inserted into straws.

CLAY CONSTRUCTION

1 Pinch off gumball-sized pieces of clay and roll them into balls (make about ten at once).

2 Insert toothpicks into the clay to build intricate structures, connecting the toothpicks with other balls of clay.

CARDBOARD CREATIONS

1 Cut cardboard into various shapes. Trace each shape onto another piece of cardboard and cut out a second symmetrical shape.

2 Wrap a strip of duct tape around the edge of each piece. Trim excess tape from the ends.

3 Cut small wedges out of each side.

4 Join the pieces together perpendicularly by inserting the wedge cuts into each other to make a joint.

SKY

High Flyer

Biplane Bookshelf

Airplane Control Tower

Propeller Bling

Say It in Skywriting

Whirlybird

Bubbly Propeller Hat

Hot-Air Balloon Hanger

Daring Skydiver

Parts of a **HELICOPTER** and an **AIRPLANE**

HELICOPTER

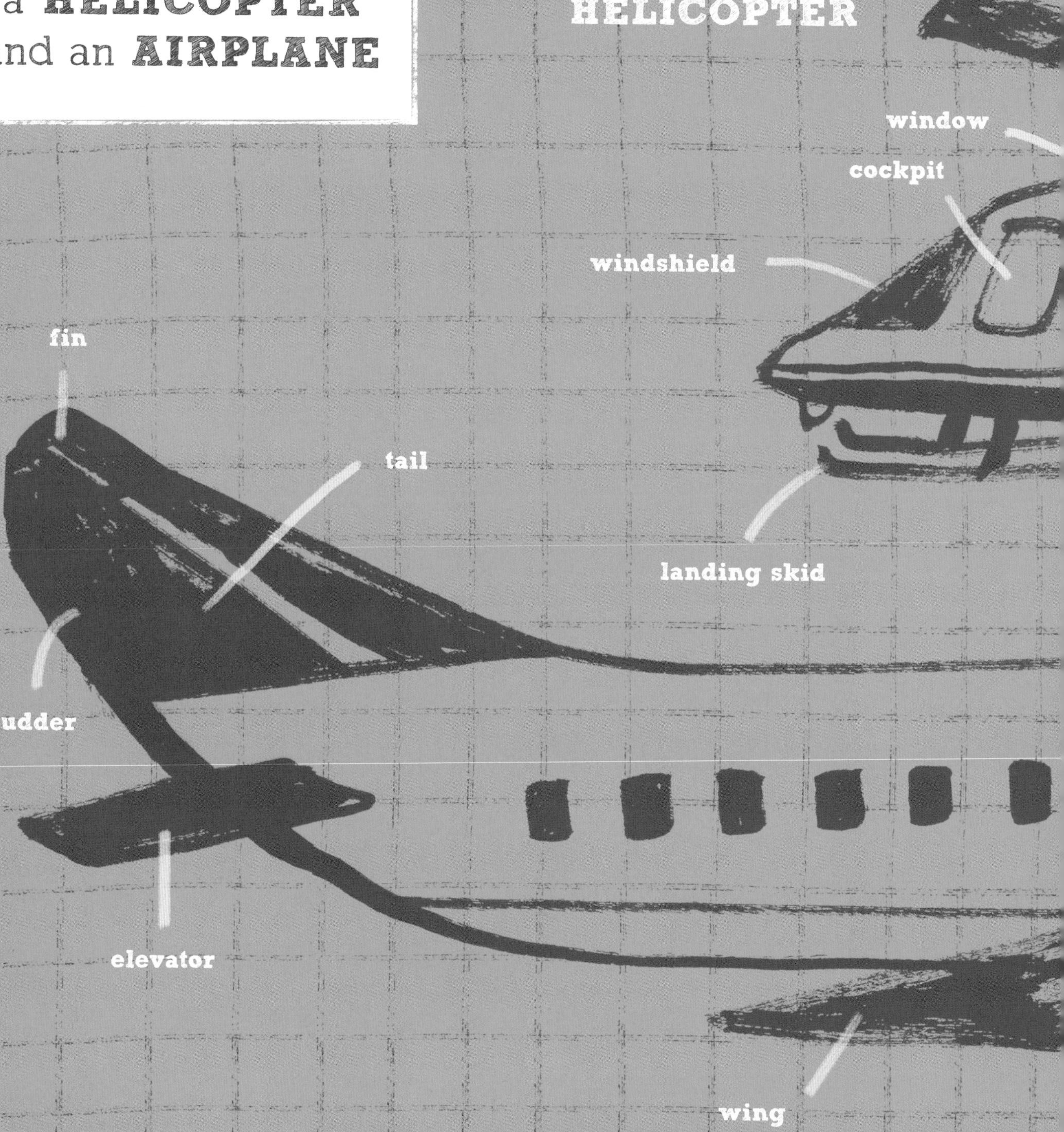

window

cockpit

windshield

fin

tail

landing skid

rudder

elevator

wing

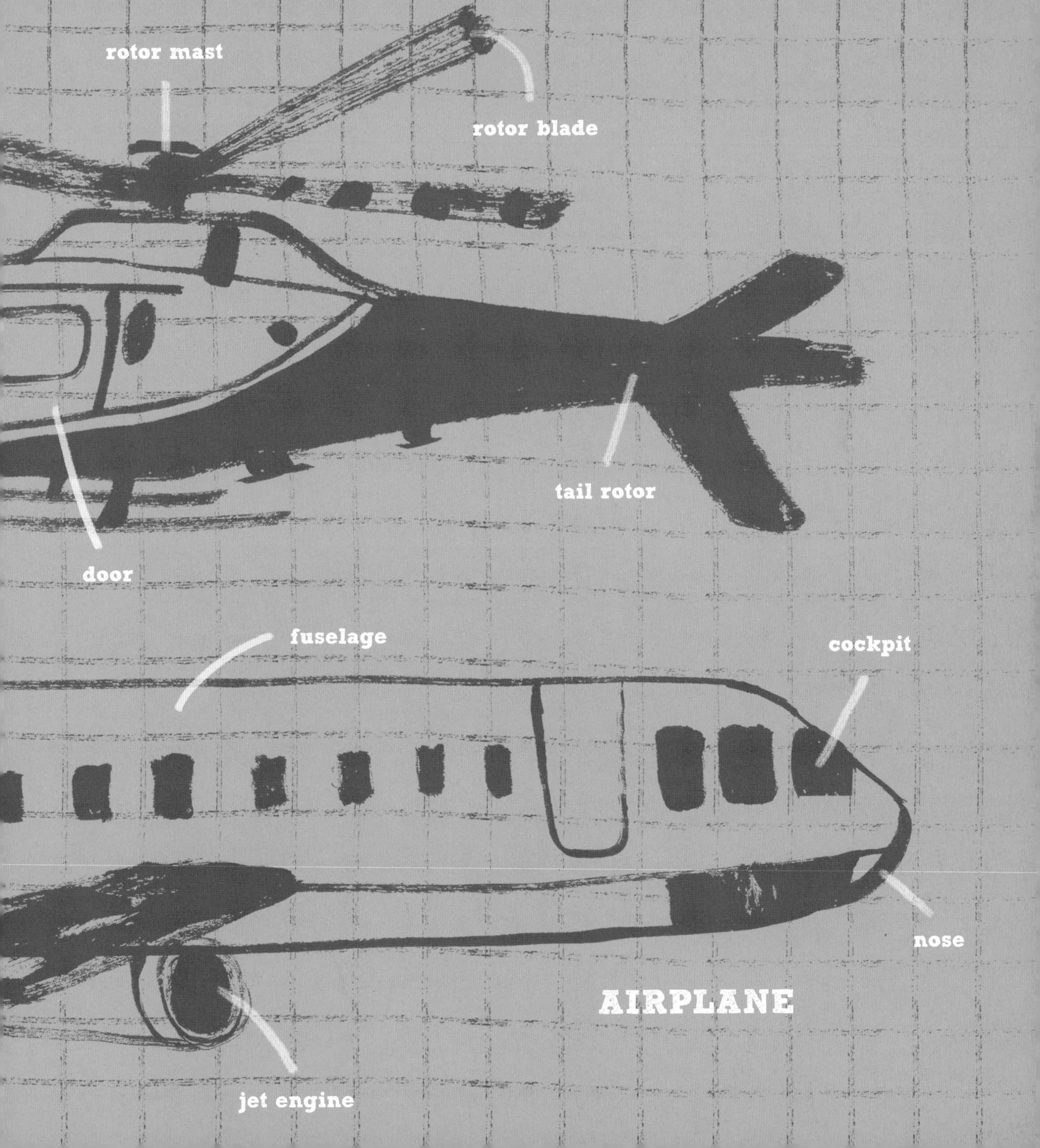

rotor mast

rotor blade

tail rotor

door

fuselage

cockpit

nose

AIRPLANE

jet engine

HIGH FLYER

Prepare for landing! Set up a zip line for your little pilot to ground his plane over and over again.

WHAT YOU'LL NEED

- Two 1-inch wooden spools
- 1 wavy wooden craft stick (available from Michaels.com)
- One 2-by-2½-inch piece of cardboard
- 1 wooden ice cream spoon
- White and mint-green paint
- Paintbrush
- One 6-inch square of origami paper
- Scissors
- 1 toilet paper tube
- Tacky glue
- Large binder clip
- 1 plastic egg
- 1 straw
- Thin silver washi tape
- Hot-glue gun
- String

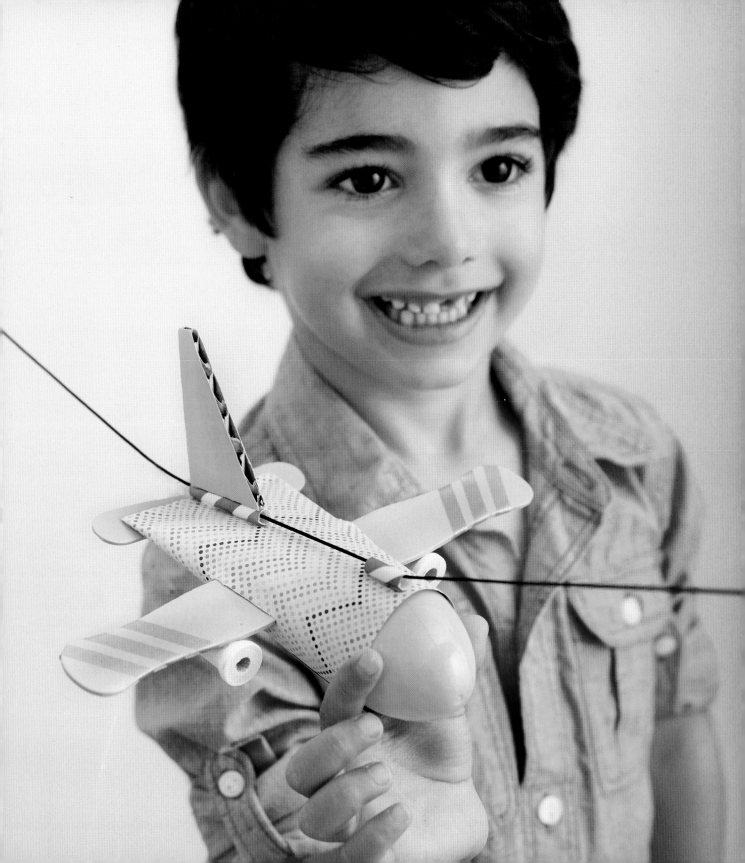

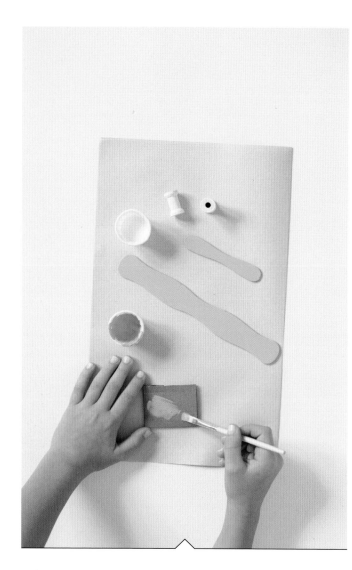

1 Paint the spools white and one side of the wavy craft stick, cardboard, and ice cream spoon mint green. Let dry and repeat on the other side of the craft stick, cardboard, and spoon.

2 While the paint is drying, cut a 1½-inch strip off the origami paper and discard. Wrap the paper around the cardboard tube and glue to secure.

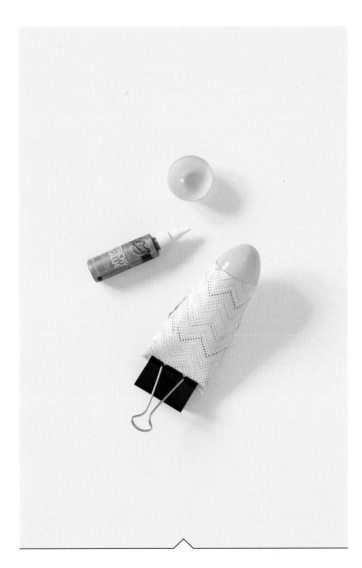

3 Glue one end of the tube shut and hold it together with a binder clip until dry. Glue the pointier half of the plastic egg into the other end of the tube, rounded side out, to make the plane's **nose**.

 To make the plane's **wings**, have an adult cut a 1-inch slit on either side of the tube and push the wavy craft stick through until it's even on both sides. Add the **jet engines**: glue a wooden spool below the wing on either side of the airplane's **fuselage** (body).

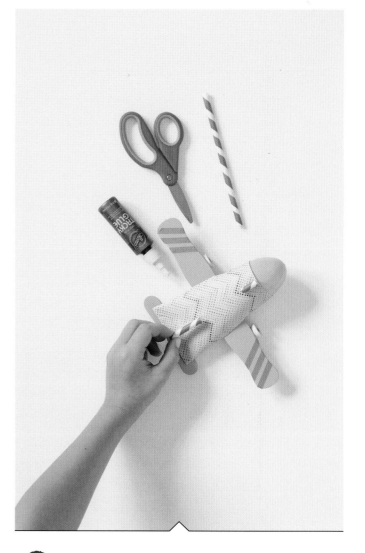

5 Remove the binder clip from the plane and glue the ice cream spoon underneath the back edge to make the **elevator**.

6 Cut the straw into a ½-inch piece and a 2-inch piece. Glue the small piece to the top front edge of the plane, close to the plane's nose, and glue the longer one at the very back edge of the plane. Add three diagonal stripes of washi tape on both wings.

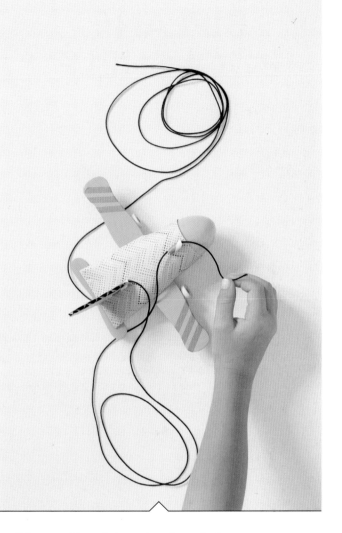

7

To make the plane's **rudder**, cut the painted piece of cardboard in half diagonally and discard one half. Have an adult hot-glue the bottom edge of the cardboard triangle to the top of the back straw segment with the diagonal edge facing the nose of the plane.

Thread the string through the straw segments and then tape or tie the ends of the string to two points in the room, preferably in an open corner.

BIPLANE BOOKSHELF

Take your library to new heights with a few simple tricks.

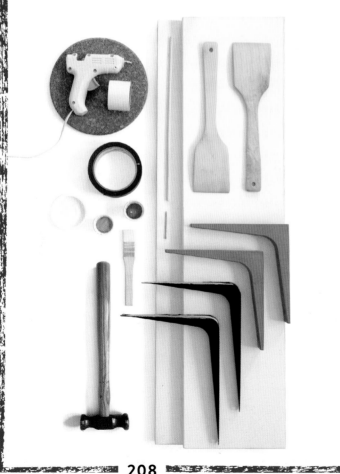

WHAT YOU'LL NEED

- Two 32-by-8-inch shelves

- 4 brackets: 2 colored, 2 painted to match your wall

- Hanging hardware to suit your walls

- 2 wooden spatulas with holes in the handles

- Painter's tape

- Red and blue acrylic paint

- Paintbrush

- Hot-glue gun

- One 6-inch cork trivet

- 1 long nail

- Drill (optional)

- Hammer

- 1 white Play-Doh lid

1 Mount the top shelf to the wall using the colored brackets. Mount the brackets that match your wall for the lower shelf so that there's about an inch between the bottom edge of the colored bracket and the top of the bottom shelf.

2 To make the propeller, stick two diagonal strips of tape to the ends of both spatulas, then paint to create stripes. Remove the tape and let dry.

3 Have an adult hot-glue the spatulas in a straight line, lining up the holes.

4 Have an adult poke a hole in the center of the cork trivet with a nail and remove. Insert the nail into the spatula holes and then back into the cork trivet. Hammer this nail into the front middle edge of the shelf. (You can predrill a hole to prevent the wood from splitting.) Have an adult hot-glue the Play-Doh lid over the nail head to create the plane's nose.

These shelves are hung on a chalkboard-painted wall, with landing gear drawn on in white chalk, but you can replicate the effect with strips of black masking tape.

WHOOSH!

AIRPLANE CONTROL TOWER

The air traffic control tower keeps airplanes from colliding in the sky. It's like a traffic cop in the air!

WHAT YOU'LL NEED

- 1 paper towel tube
- White paint
- Paintbrush
- Red washi tape
- Tacky glue
- 1 bottle or jar lid (larger in diameter than the paper towel tube)
- One 32-ounce wide plastic drink bottle (mine was a Powerade bottle)
- Scissors
- Electrical tape
- Hot-glue gun
- 1 wooden skewer
- Nail
- One ½- to 1-inch wooden bead
- Black card stock
- 1 straw
- 24-gauge jewelry wire
- Wire cutters
- Toy figurine (optional)

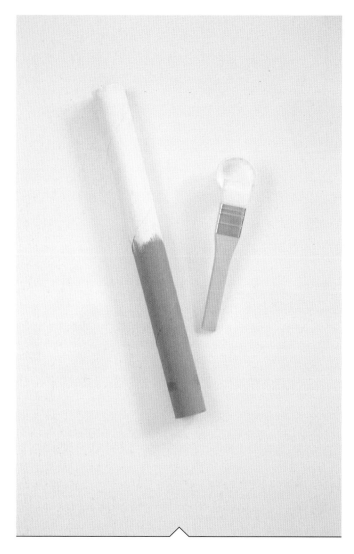

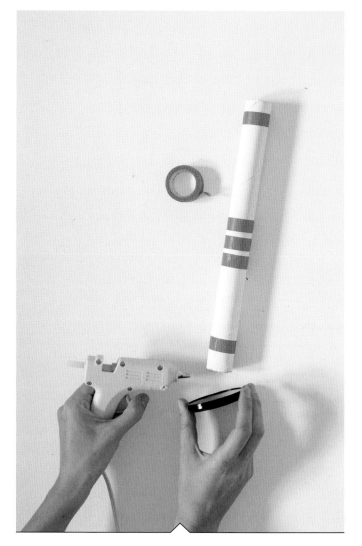

 Paint the paper towel tube white.

 Once the tube is dry, add five horizontal stripes of red washi tape as shown. Glue one end of the tube to the inside of the jar lid and set aside to dry.

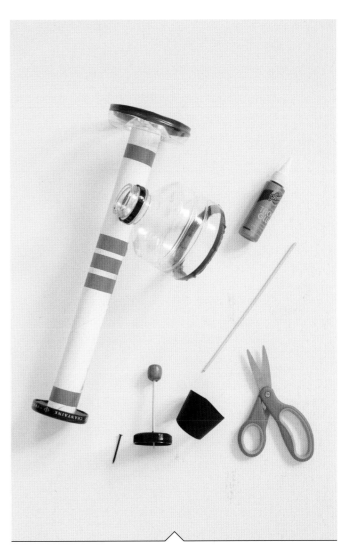

3 Have an adult cut 1 inch off the bottom of the drink bottle and then cut about 4 inches off the top part of the bottle. Cover the cut edges of both the top and bottom of the bottle with electrical tape. Have an adult hot-glue the bottom portion of the bottle to the other end of the paper towel tube.

4 Cut a 3-inch piece off the skewer. (If you score the skewer by just barely cutting into it with scissors, it will snap cleanly when you break it.) Have an adult push a nail through the cap of the bottle and insert the skewer into the hole (pointy side going into the cap); glue to secure in place. Glue a bead on top of the skewer and twist the top back on the bottle. Cut a 1-inch-wide strip of black card stock and wrap it into a slightly conical shape around the cap; tape the seam.

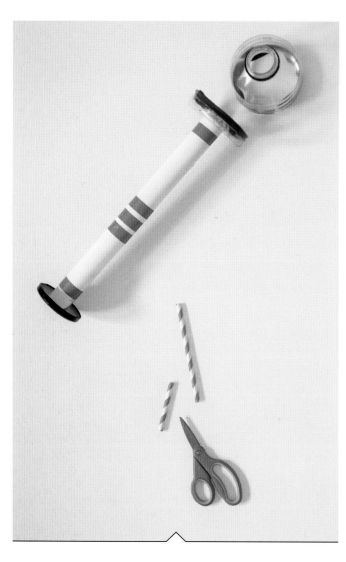

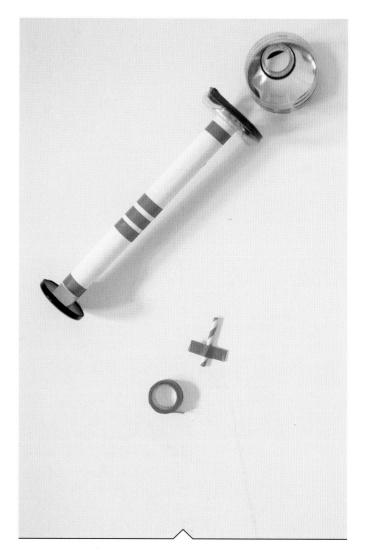

5 To make an airplane, cut a 2-inch piece of the straw (this will be the plane's **fuselage**).

6 To make the **wings**, center a 4-inch strip of red washi tape about ¼ inch from one end, then fold the ends back in on themselves and adhere them next to the straw.

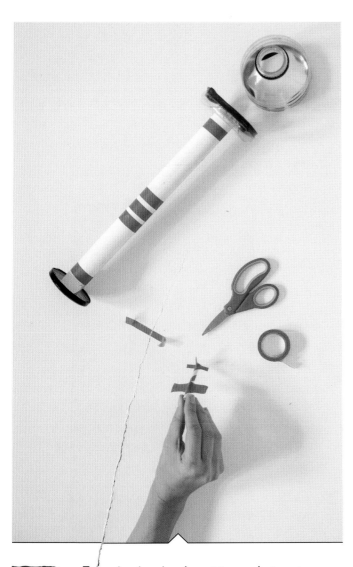

7 To make the plane's **rudder** and **elevator**, take a 4-inch piece of tape, cut it in half lengthwise, and center it on the opposite end of the fuselage, pinching it to create the **fin** and then folding the ends underneath.

8 Have an adult use wire cutters to cut a 10-inch piece of wire. Squeeze a dot of glue into the back end of the straw and then squeeze the straw closed around the wire. Let dry and twist the opposite end of the wire around the neck of the bottle. Repeat to make as many planes as you'd like.

PROPELLER BLING

Did you know that the more blades a propeller has, the quieter it is? This three-blade ring won't disturb your neighbors in science class.

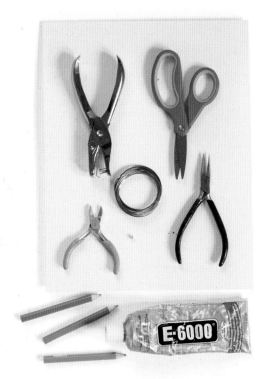

WHAT YOU'LL NEED

- Propeller template (download at ProjectKid.com/propeller)
- Computer, printer, and printer paper
- Scissors
- Shrinky Dinks paper
- Markers or **colored pencils**
- ¼-inch hole punch
- 24-gauge wire
- Wire cutters
- Needle-nose pliers
- 1 small bead
- E-6000 glue

1 Download and print the propeller template. Cut it out and trace it onto the Shrinky Dinks paper. Color the propeller and cut it out. Punch a hole in the center.

2 Bake in the oven according to package directions. Let cool for 5 to 10 minutes.

3 Have an adult cut a 4-inch piece of wire with wire cutters and twist it around the child's finger, using needle-nose pliers to hold the end of the wire while wrapping. (Don't twist too tight; you want to be able to slip the ring on and off.) Leave a ¼-inch twisted point.

4 Slip the propeller on top of the wire point, and then have an adult glue the bead onto the wire point with E-6000 glue. Let dry, about 20 minutes. Have an adult trim any excess wire.

SAY IT IN SKYWRITING

Bring the magic of skywriting to your door with a message that *won't* disappear.

WHAT YOU'LL NEED

- Computer, printer, and printer paper
- Tape
- 24-gauge floral wire
- Wire cutters
- Parchment paper
- White pom-poms in various sizes (no larger than ½ inch)
- Quick-dry tacky glue
- String
- Scissors

FOR THE PAPER AIRPLANE

- One 5-by-7-inch piece of red paper

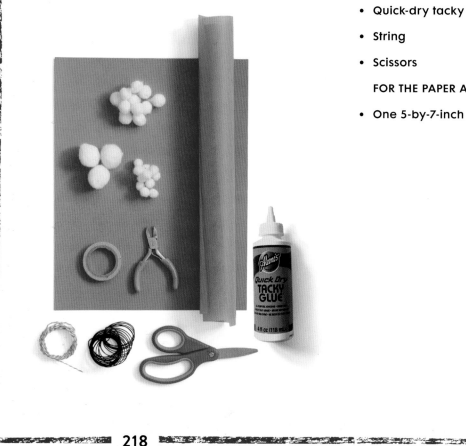

1 Print out a word or name in a simple script font so that the letters are about 3 inches tall (I used Pacifico, 330 point, for a six-letter name). Tape the printout onto your work surface and form the wire into the word, following the printout as a guide. Once you have each letter formed how you want it, twist the wire to keep it in place. Have an adult use wire cutters to snip the wire, leaving about 3 inches at the end of the word or name.

2 Place the wire on parchment paper and begin gluing pom-poms to it, varying the sizes of the pom-poms as you work down its length. Don't worry about the glue dripping onto the paper; the waxy surface will allow for an easy release. Let the glue dry completely.

 Fold an airplane out of the red paper (turn the page for the how-to) and glue it to the end of the wire.

 Cut a piece of string about 24 inches long and tie each end to a point along the word or name and hang.

 Fold a 5-by-7-inch piece of paper in half lengthwise and crease it sharply. Unfold the paper. Fold the top left corner of the paper down to meet the crease. Repeat for the top right corner.

2 Now fold the two top diagonal side edges toward the center line.

Fold in half on the crease, so the folds are on the inside. Take one flap and fold it outward to meet the center crease.

Flip over and repeat on the other side.

WHIRLYBIRD

If this helicopter needs to make a crash landing, its soft exterior will protect it from major damage.

WHAT YOU'LL NEED

- One 3-inch Styrofoam ball
- Yellow yarn
- Black and orange felt
- Scissors
- Tacky glue
- 2 tongue depressors
- 1 golf tee
- 2 wooden ice cream spoons
- 1 wooden coffee stirrer
- 2 large bobby pins
- Hot-glue gun

BONUS PROJECT:
Make the helicopter's
landing pad by stenciling
the letter "H" onto a circular
cardboard coaster.

 Wrap the Styrofoam ball in yarn until it is fully covered. To make the **windshield**, cut a 4-inch-diameter circle from black felt; cut the circle in half and round the sharp corners on one half; discard the other. Glue the half-circle onto one side of the yarn ball. To make the helicopter's **door**, cut a 2-by-1-inch rectangle from black felt and glue it next to the semicircle. Glue a small rectangle of orange felt, about ½ by ¾ inch, on top of it to make the door's **window**.

 To make the **rotor blades**, glue the tongue depressors in an X formation. Glue them to the top of the golf tee (this will be the **rotor mast**). Set aside to dry. Make the helicopter's **tail rotor** by cutting one ice cream spoon in half and gluing the cut edges of the two pieces to one end of the other spoon to make a V shape.

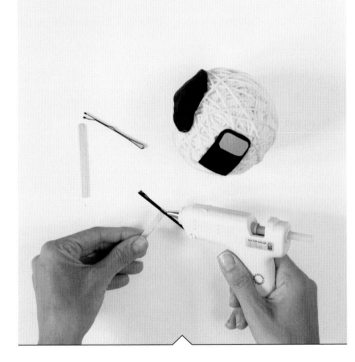

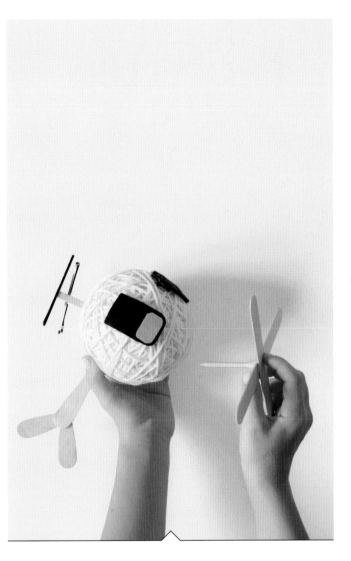

3 To make the **landing skids**, break the coffee stirrer in half. Have an adult hot-glue the ends of the two pieces in between the arms of the bobby pins to form a T. Push the other ends of the stirrer pieces up into the bottom of the helicopter.

4 Insert the tail into the back of the helicopter. Insert the golf tee into the top of the yarn ball. (You can glue it if you choose, but leaving it loose allows it to spin.)

BUBBLY PROPELLER HAT

Inspector Gadget has nothing on you with this bubble-powered flying machine!

WHAT YOU'LL NEED

- One 6-inch-diameter paper bowl
- Pencil
- Paint
- Paintbrush
- Thin twine or string
- Scissors
- Six 1-inch buttons
- 4 bubble wands
- ¼-inch hole punch
- Elastic cord
- Paracord (available from Michaels.com)
- 2 empty bubble solution bottles
- Hammer and nail
- Colored duct tape

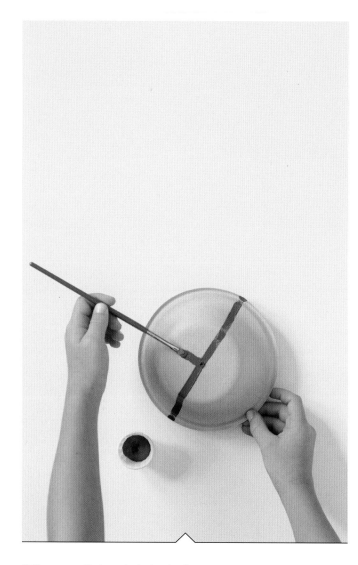

1 Poke a hole in the bottom center of the bowl with a pencil. Paint stripes, dots, or zigzags on the bowl to decorate.

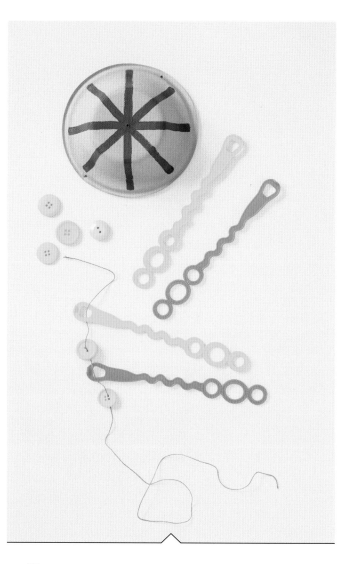

2 Cut a 12-inch piece of string. Thread the string up through one buttonhole, then through the handle of the first bubble wand, then through another button, and so on until you've made a stack of five buttons and four bubble wands, with a button on the top and on the bottom.

 Go back down the stack, threading the string through the opposite hole on each button as you go down.

4 Insert the two string tails into the hole on the painted side of the bowl. Thread the tails through two holes in another button and tie a knot to secure.

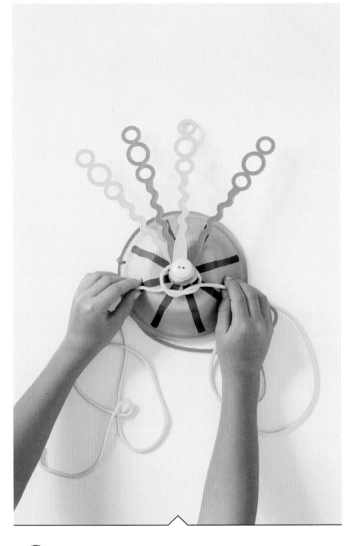

5 To make a chin strap for your hat, punch a hole on either side of the bowl and knot a piece of elastic cord through both holes. (Make sure it's tight enough to keep the hat on but isn't uncomfortable.)

6 Cut an approximately 5-foot-long piece of paracord and tie the middle of the cord around the bottom button of the propeller, where it meets the bowl. (Adjust the length of the cord according to the arm length of the child.)

7 Have an adult use a hammer and nail to punch holes in the tops of both bubble solution bottle caps. Thread the end of one of the cords through the hole in one cap; knot on the underside of the cap. Reseal the bottle. Repeat with the second bottle and cord.

8 Decorate the bubble bottles with tape, then suit up in the apparatus to take flight.

HOT-AIR BALLOON HANGER

If you can't find a bouncy ball exactly this size, just make sure you get a hoop that's slightly smaller than the ball's circumference.

WHAT YOU'LL NEED

- One 15-inch-diameter rubber ball
- 3 colors of thin washi tape
- Fishing line
- Scissors
- One 14-inch-diameter embroidery hoop (the inner, solid ring)
- Twine
- 1-inch-wide ribbon
- Permanent glue dots
- 1 wooden berry container
- Pom-pom fringe
- 1 ceiling hook
- Hot-glue gun

Did you know that the
hot-air balloon is the oldest
vehicle to successfully carry
people in the air?

Stick a strip of washi tape to a point in the middle of the ball and wrap it halfway around the ball. Create an X shape by crossing over this line with another piece of washi tape, starting and stopping along the same imaginary line going around the middle of the ball. Continue bisecting each section of the X, alternating colors, until you've added about twenty pieces of tape.

 Decide how far from the ceiling you'd like your balloon to hang and cut four pieces of fishing line accordingly. Tie the fishing line at evenly spaced points around the embroidery hoop. Tie four 24-inch pieces of twine to the same points. Gather the twine pieces together and tie them in a knot about 20 inches below the hoop.

 Use glue dots to attach pom-pom fringe around the top edge of the berry basket.

6 Gather the fishing line strands above the ball. Knot together and hang from the ceiling hook. Rest the basket on top of the twine knot. Make sure it's level and then have an adult hot-glue it in place.

3 Cut a 44-inch piece of ribbon. Use glue dots to attach the ribbon around the embroidery hoop, covering the twine and fishing line knots.

4 Rest the ball in the embroidery hoop, lining up the hoop with the ends of the tape. Fit the ball in the hoop snugly.

DARING SKYDIVER

Ready, set . . . JUMP! Make a bunch of these daredevils and hang them from your ceiling or attach them to sticks to make an adorable mobile.

WHAT YOU'LL NEED

- 1 balloon
- Mod Podge, glossy
- Foam brush
- Newsprint, ripped into 1-inch-square pieces
- Scissors
- 1¾-inch paper punch
- 2 or more colors of paint
- Small paintbrush
- ⅛-inch hole punch
- Small beads (at least ¼-inch)
- String
- Small doll or figurine (3 to 4 inches tall)
- Nail or other small sharp object
- Twine

1 Inflate the balloon to 4 to 6 inches in diameter. Beginning at the top of the balloon, coat it in 4-inch-square sections with Mod Podge using a foam brush. Place newsprint pieces on top of the Mod Podge, and then generously cover the paper with more Mod Podge. Keep covering about a quarter of the way down the sides of the balloon with overlapping newsprint pieces until a shallow bowl-like shape is formed.

2 Cut a 2-inch-wide strip of newsprint and use the paper punch to create a reverse-scalloped edge. Mod Podge the strip around the edge of the completed parachute shape, smoothing down the paper. Then add two more layers of newsprint on top of the dome. Let it dry overnight, or until it feels like a hard shell when you tap it. (I stood my balloon knot-side down in a roll of duct tape to dry.)

3 Pop the balloon with scissors, peel off the latex from inside the bowl, and throw away the latex. Trim off any excess dried Mod Podge around the reverse-scalloped edge. Paint your parachute to your liking, using the points as a guide for where your stripes go. (I chose two colors per parachute, leaving one strip natural.)

4 Punch holes at each point in the scalloped edge with the ⅛-inch hole punch. Cut a 12-inch-long string for each point. Knot a small bead to one end of each string, and thread it through each hole, with the bead on the inside. Knot all of the strings together at the bottom and slip the jumper's arms over the knot. Have an adult use a nail to poke a hole in the top center of the parachute. Suspend the parachute with a bead knotted to a length of twine, as described above.

SPACE

*

Parts of
a
ROCKET

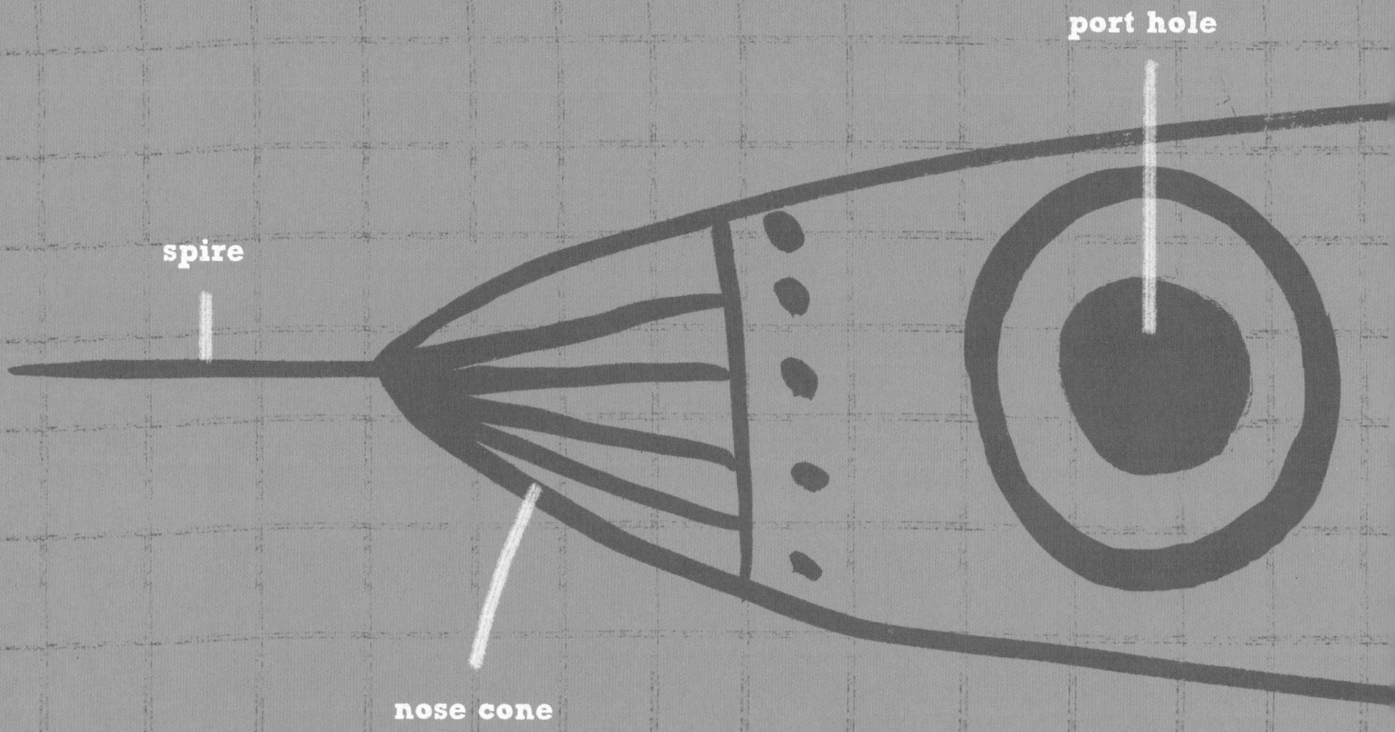

port hole

spire

nose cone

fuselage

HANGING ROCKET HIDEAWAY

This no-sew project creates the ideal place for planning the playground you'll build on Mars.

WHAT YOU'LL NEED

- Queen- or full-sized flat white bedsheet
- Scissors
- Painter's tape
- Black acrylic paint
- Paintbrush
- Black permanent marker
- Ruler
- Black ink pad
- Wine cork
- Towel
- Black, blue, and red felt
- Fabric glue
- 3-inch-wide black ribbon
- 2 Hula-hoops
- Stapler
- Fishing line

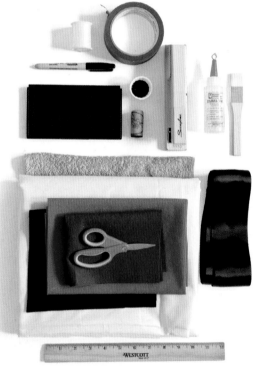

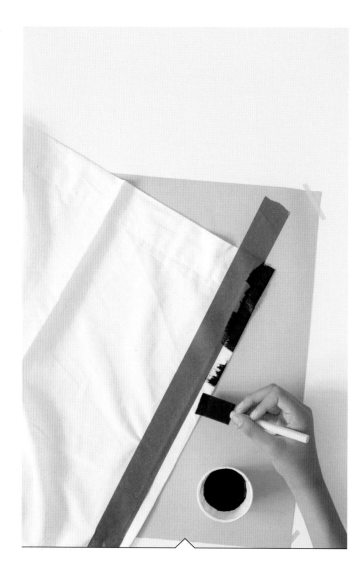

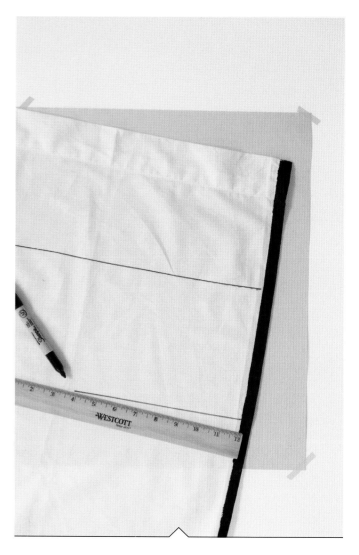

 Cut the sheet from the bottom so it measures about 80 inches tall. With the wide hem of the sheet on top of your work surface, adhere painter's tape on the outside of each of the two narrower hems and paint a black line, about ¾ inch wide, on each hem. Let dry.

Lay the sheet flat on the floor and draw horizontal lines from one side to the other. These lines create the "metal panels" that come together to make up the **fuselage**. Let your NASA engineer draw additional horizontal and vertical lines to create his own panels, dividing up the sheet into five to eight sections.

3 To create the rivets, use a cork to stamp circles on either side of each line, 2 to 3 inches apart. Place the towel under the sheet before stamping to create a cushion. Dab the cork a number of times to make sure it has enough ink on it before pressing it onto the fabric.

4 Cut 8- to 10-inch letters spelling USA from black felt. Use fabric glue to attach these to the rocket vertically near one of the ¾-inch vertical lines at the tent's opening, about 1 foot from the cut bottom edge (see the photo on page 247).

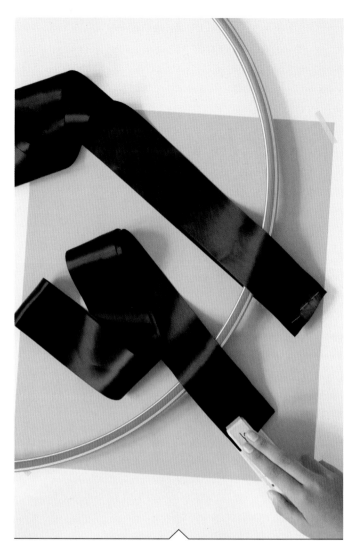

5 To make the flag, cut a 3-by-5-inch rectangle of blue felt and seven red felt stripes, three that are 1 inch by 4 inches and four that are 1 inch by 7 inches. Glue to the top third of the sheet, opposite USA, with fabric glue, leaving ½-inch spaces between the shapes.

6 To make the **nose cone**, cut twelve 4-foot lengths of ribbon. Loop each one through a Hula-hoop and staple the ends together. Thread a 12-inch piece of ribbon through all of the loops at the inside of the hoop and secure with a knot.

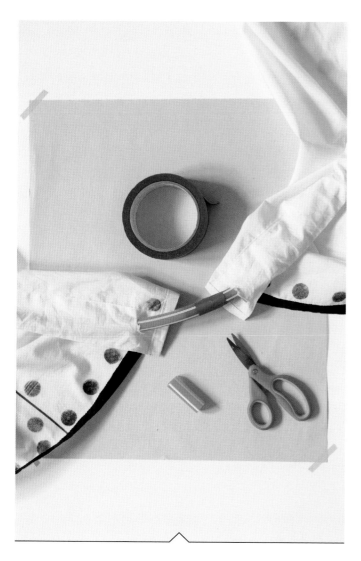

7 Cut about 1 inch off the second Hula-hoop. Cut a slit on the inside corners of the top of the sheet and feed the hoop through the seam at the top of the sheet. Reconnect the ends of the hoop using a piece of tape.

8 Stack the ribbon hoop under the sheet hoop, pull the ribbon loops through to give the nose a conical point, and hang with fishing line.

ROCKET CONTROL PANEL

Search every nook and cranny of your recycling bin, craft room, and junk drawer to find switches, knobs, and gears to help you blast off!

WHAT YOU'LL NEED

- One 18-by-24-inch pegboard
- Silver paint
- Paintbrush
- 10 feet of paracord (available from Michaels .com)
- Scissors
- Hot-glue gun (optional)
- Everything but the kitchen sink! We used . . .

  - Pipe cleaners
  - A kitchen timer
  - Jar lids
  - Old film reels
  - Marbles
  - Beads
  - Spools
  - Buttons

  - Spring doorstops
  - Screws
  - Silver duct tape
  - Ping-Pong balls
  - Gift boxes
  - Paint
  - Light switches

1

Paint one side of the pegboard silver and let dry. While the paint is drying, send your space explorer around the house to find objects to use as switches and knobs.

2

Cut the paracord into four pieces: two 48-inch and two 36-inch sections. Now "stitch" the paracord around the edges of the board (using the smaller pieces on the short sides and the long pieces on the longer sides): Knot one end of the cord and thread it through a hole on a corner of the pegboard, starting on the unpainted side of the board. Stitch the cord around the outside edge and come back in through the next hole on the unpainted side. Tie a knot on the unpainted side of the board when you reach the end of the side. Repeat for the other three sides.

5

To make a ball gearshift, put a doorstop through a hole in the board and use a nut to secure it on the back side of the board. Wrap the ends of the screw with a generous amount of duct tape. Have an adult poke a hole in a painted Ping-Pong ball with scissors and slip it over the end of the doorstop.

6

To make a light-switch panel, paint a 4-by-5-inch gift box and wrap the sides in silver duct tape. Have an adult cut a hole in the box so that the back of the switch can fit snugly inside it. Have an adult hot-glue the box edges to the board.

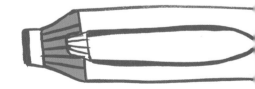

Start designing your panel. Use pipe cleaners as wires to hold to the board objects such as a kitchen timer, jar lids, old film reels, and marbles.

 To make a spool knob, thread a bead onto a pipe cleaner and pull it to the middle of the pipe cleaner. Bend the pipe cleaner in half and thread both ends through the spool. Place the spool on the board over a hole and insert both ends of the pipe cleaner into the hole. Wind the ends around a bead or a button on the other side of the board to prevent it from pulling back through.

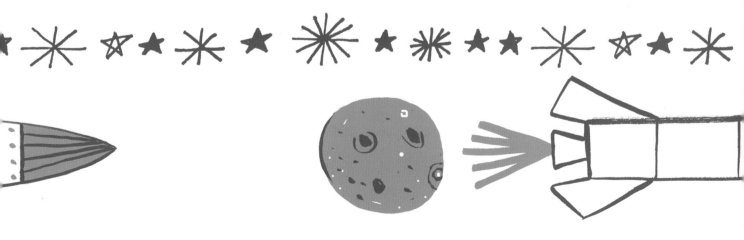

PRETEND PLANETARIUM

A twinkling string of stars and planets will send you out of this world!

WHAT YOU'LL NEED

- Polymer clay in various colors
- Rolling pin or smooth glass jar
- Small glass bowls
- Pencil
- Cookie sheet
- Paper clips
- White twinkle lights

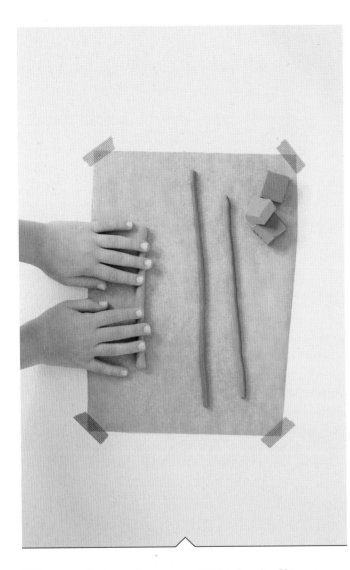

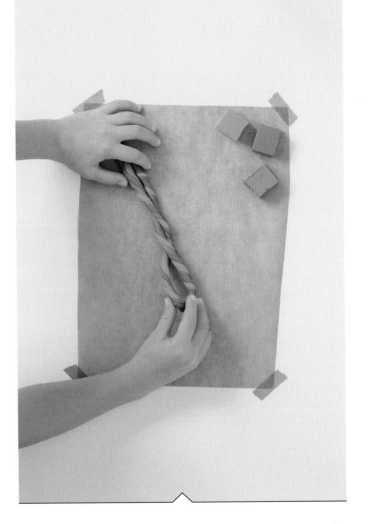

1 Preheat the oven to 275°F. Pinch off two to four quarter-sized pieces of clay, in various colors. Roll each into a long "snake." Stack the snakes together and roll them into one thick striped snake. Twist it to make a spiral swirl with the colors.

2 Bend this spiral in half and twist the two ends together, then roll it out again into a snake. Repeat two or three times until you have the marbled blend of colors you are trying to achieve. Roll the clay into a ball and then flatten it with your rolling pin until it's about ¼ inch thick.

Place a small glass bowl on top of the clay and trace around it with a pencil, going all the way through the clay to cut it into a perfect circle. Use the pencil to poke a small hole about ¼ inch from the edge of the circle. Drape each clay circle over the bottom of a glass bowl and smooth down. (This gives your planet a dome-like shape.)

Repeat steps 1 through 3 using different combinations of clay to make as many planets as you'd like. Place the bowls on a cookie sheet and bake in the oven for 15 minutes. Let cool completely and then lift the clay domes off of the bowls. Thread paper clips through the holes in the clay planets and hang on the white twinkle lights.

SPACE RANGER HELMET & GOGGLES

To discover alien life-forms lurking in unseen places, design this special exploration gear.

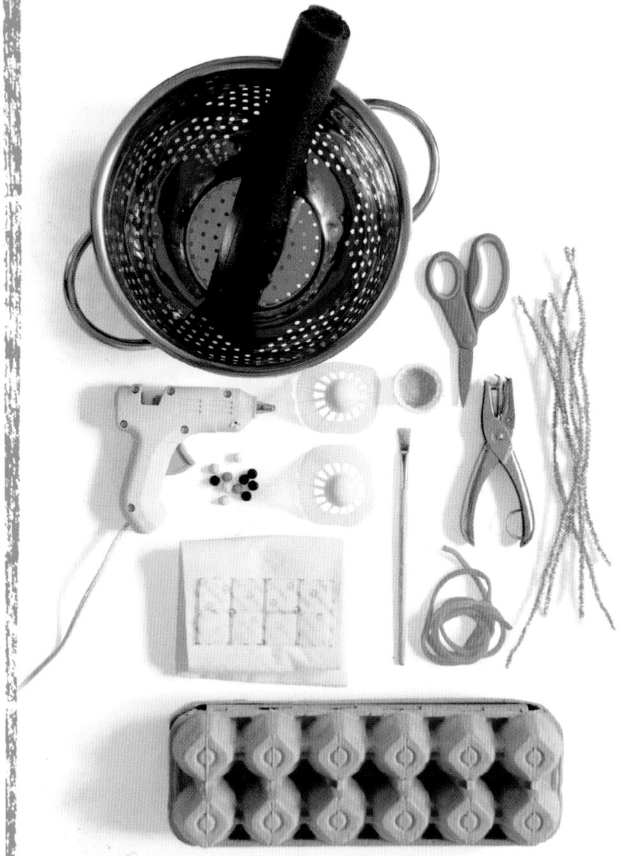

WHAT YOU'LL NEED

FOR THE HELMET

- 1 quart-sized metal colander
- Silver pipe cleaners
- Beads in various sizes
- 1½-inch-diameter foam pipe insulation
- Scissors
- Felt
- Adhesive velcro

FOR THE GOGGLES

- 2 shuttlecocks
- Scissors
- 1 egg carton
- ¼-inch hole punch
- Silver paint
- Paintbrush
- Hot-glue gun
- Elastic cord

HELMET

 1 Thread pipe cleaners through the holes in the colander at random to create a wacky helmet radar setup. Slip beads onto the pipe cleaners for extra-superstrength alien detection powers. Fold, bend, and twist the pipe cleaners to make sure they stay in place.

 2 Once the circuits are in place, cut two 3-inch segments of pipe insulation. Use pipe cleaners to wire them to the inside bottom of the colander (top of the helmet). Space explorers need to be comfortable!

 **3** To create the helmet's chin strap, cut a 1-by-14-inch piece of felt and adhere a tab of the rough Velcro to either end on the same side of the strap. Two inches down from the rough Velcro on either side of the strap, attach a 3-inch strip of soft Velcro (to allow the strap to be adjustable). Thread the strap through the colander's handles.

GOGGLES

 1 Cut the ends off of the shuttlecocks to create openings that are 1½ inches in diameter. (Save the points of the shuttlecock for another craft project.) Cut out two segments of the egg carton, keeping them connected. Have an adult cut holes in the center of each segment that are a bit smaller than 1½ inches in diameter.

 **3** Have an adult hot-glue the shuttlecock segments around the holes in the egg carton. Cut the elastic cord to fit around the child's head, then knot the elastic through the two holes.

 2 Punch a hole on either side of the egg carton piece for the elastic cord. Paint the egg carton piece and let dry.

SUPER SPACE ROCKET

Before heading to his job at NASA, your engineer can practice his tinkering skills on this mini rocket.

WHAT YOU'LL NEED

- 1 mini tart tin
- 1 empty aerosol sunscreen bottle
- Hot-glue gun
- Silver duct tape
- Colored electrical tape
- Black ½-inch letter and number stickers
- 5-by-7-inch piece of paper
- Scissors
- Zip tie (optional)

1 Have an adult hot-glue the bottom of the tart tin to the bottom of the bottle.

2 Decorate the bottle with silver duct tape and colored electrical tape. Use letter and number stickers to add the name of the rocket to the side of the bottle.

3 To make the rocket's **nose cone**, cover the piece of paper with two or three rows of 6-inch-long strips of silver duct tape, aligned side by side. Cut a 3-inch-tall-by-5-inch-wide semicircle out of the taped paper and roll it into a cone. Use a piece of the duct tape to secure. Trim the open edge so that it's even all around.

4 If you wish to give your rocket a **spire**, insert a zip tie into the top hole of the cone. Have an adult hot-glue the cone over the nozzle of the bottle.

A Crafter's Toolbox

Part of what I hope to do in this book is to simplify what materials you'll use, when to use them, and why I recommend them. Use these pages as a reference when embarking on any craft project.

ADHESIVES

- **Hot-glue gun:** An adults-only tool that creates an instantaneous strong bond; the best cure for impatient young crafters who are allergic to drying time.
- **Tacky glue:** A great all-purpose adhesive that's stronger than school glue but safer than hot glue.
- **Glue dots:** Quick, clean, and kid-friendly, they come in different strengths, from repositionable to permanent.
- **Glue stick:** Best used for a paper-to-paper bond.
- **E-6000 glue:** A stinky cement-like glue. Pull out this big gun on those rare occasions when hot glue isn't bonding.
- **Wood glue:** Self-explanatory, right?
- **School glue:** Can hold a bit beyond paper, but doesn't respond as well to gravity.
- **Fabric glue:** It's all in the name.
- **Mod Podge:** An adhesive and topcoat used in decoupage.

TAPES

- **Colored masking tape:** Rip-able, thick, and affordable for striping or covering large areas.
- **Washi tape:** The foreign-exchange student of tape—exotic, colorful, and surprising, but rarely permanent.
- **Duct tape:** Strong and sturdy . . . can turn even the flimsiest of papers into an indestructible surface.
- **Double-stick tape:** You don't need any help with this one.
- **Clear tape:** An office-supply staple.
- **Electrical tape:** A rubbery and stretchy tape that enjoys going around curves.

CUTTING TOOLS

- **Kid scissors:** Have a bunch of these on hand for playdates and birthday parties.
- **Adult scissors:** Use your grown-up muscle to cut through things like wooden craft sticks.
- **Utility knife:** Sometimes cardboard, foam core, or balsa wood needs this adults-only tool.
- **Wire clippers:** Not necessary for pipe cleaners, but best to use these adults-only cutters on other types of wire.
- **Decorative-edge scissors:** Shears that create zigzagged, scalloped, wavy, or deckled edges.
- **Hole punch:** Imperative for garland making, DIY lacing cards, and all things hole-y.

PAINTS & BRUSHES

- **Acrylic paint:** Thick with good coverage, but permanent—so bring out the smocks!
- **Tempera paint:** A washable option that's great for little ones (and particularly well-suited to paper crafts).
- **Fabric paint:** Best for wearable projects, as it doesn't stiffen the fabric.
- **Dimensional fabric paint:** Aka puffy paint, this 1980s fave can be used on paper, fabric, and hard surfaces like wood, glass, and plastic.

- **Watercolor paint:** For the more delicate of young crafters. You can teach them the technique mantra: Water, paint, paper. Water, paint, paper.
- **Foam paintbrushes:** Very inexpensive and can really take a beating from the youngest of makers.

FIBERS

- **Yarn:** Soft and affordable; comes in many weights and textures.
- **Twine:** Usually made from natural fibers like hemp or jute, this is the workhorse of the string family.
- **Rope:** Adds a nautical vibe to any project, in any weight or texture.
- **Embroidery thread:** Sometimes referred to as embroidery floss, this is a favorite among friendship bracelet makers and stitchers.
- **Ribbon:** Sometimes a project just needs a soft, feminine touch to tie it all together.

PAPERS & FABRICS

- **Scrapbook paper:** Traditionally sized in 12-inch-square sheets, scrapbook paper comes double-sided, solid, textured, patterned, holiday-themed . . . you name it, they make it.
- **Newsprint:** Thin and inexpensive, a pad of newsprint isn't precious and goes a long way. Works great with papier-mâché.
- **Tissue paper:** Great for both gift-wrapping and decoupage.
- **Card stock:** Thick solid-colored paper that is often letter-sized and can run through a printer.
- **Origami paper:** Whether solid or patterned, origami paper is always square, usually 6 by 6 inches.

- **Foam core:** A sturdy and clean alternative to cardboard, for when you want a more refined look.
- **Felt:** A great fabric for beginner crafters because it comes in a variety of shades, it's sturdy, and when cut, the edges do not fray.

TRADITIONAL CRAFT SUPPLIES & TOOLS

- **Wood craft sticks:** A classic, useful building block for many, many craft projects.
- **Beads:** They can always be added to embellish a simple project.
- **Buttons:** Good for eyes, wheels, headlights, and the centers of flowers.
- **Sequins:** Not just for your ice-skating leotard! Sequins are like disks of glitter, and a whole lot easier to clean up.
- **Glitter:** Probably the most-feared craft supply. I say embrace the bling and add a bit of sparkle to your art . . . and your floorboards.
- **Craft wood shapes:** Crisp and solid shapes that can be painted, glued on, and even cut up.
- **Wooden spools:** Vintage or new, these have great versatility and can be used for everything from wheels to doll torsos.
- **Pipe cleaners:** Kids' first wire, it can be used as both a fastener and a craft material.
- **Pom-poms:** Make your own from yarn, or use store-bought poufs in a multitude of colors.
- **Craft foam:** This is a great material for toddlers when they're learning to use scissors.
- **Ink pads and rubber stamps:** Have a few alphabet and number sets on hand; these are perfect for personalizing objects that can't run through a printer.

HOUSEHOLD MATERIALS

- **Cardboard:** Don't throw away that cereal or FedEx box! It will come in handy, I promise!
- **Old clothes, sheets, and towels:** An eco-friendly source of free fabric!
- **Bottle caps:** Don't throw them away. Like ever. It will shock you how often they will make it into projects.
- **Jars:** Great for making terrariums and homemade candles. Also useful for storing craft supplies.
- **Plastic drink bottles:** Leave some room in the landfills and keep these beauties for bud vases and airplane fuselages.
- **Cardboard tubes:** From marble runs to binoculars, the possibilities are endless.
- **Corks:** Create perfect polka-dot stamps with the end of a cork.

Resources

BEADS, BELLS, AND JEWELRY-MAKING SUPPLIES AND TOOLS

Bead Center

beadcenterny.com

Whatever bead style you can possibly dream up—wood, ceramic, glass, stone—exists in this megastore of bling.

Toho Shoji

tohoshoji-ny.com

Great for jewelry findings of all sorts and miniature colorful bells.

DECORATIVE TAPE

Cutetape

cutetape.com

If you haven't jumped on the washi tape bandwagon yet, you will once you visit this site.

FABRIC

B & J Fabrics

bandjfabrics.com

From Liberty of London prints to awesome oilcloth patterns, this store has the best high/low range of fabrics you'll ever see.

The City Quilter

cityquilter.com

This store's fabrics are bright, happy, and super affordable . . . perfect for craft experiments with your kids.

Magic Cabin

magiccabin.com

With fifty-six (not a typo!) colors of 100 percent wool felt, this is my go-to spot for one of my favorite materials.

GARDEN SUPPLIES

Jamali Gardens

jamaligarden.com

If you're in need of sheet moss, seashells, or the most fabulous array of colored wire, you've got to shop here. They sell garden supplies you didn't even know existed.

GENERAL CRAFTS

American Crafts

americancrafts.com

Fresh, clean, and modern, this brand nails it every season with their new products. With adorable, happy, and kid-friendly patterns and colors, their scrapbook paper can't be beat.

Factory Direct Craft

factorydirectcraft.com

With their great prices on everything from wooden wheels to googly eyes to glitter, you'll always find a deal . . . and then some.

Michaels Craft Stores

michaels.com

My home away from home—awesome craft products, frequent sales, stylish gifts. And they sell candy. Enough said.

HARDWARE AND HOME

Bed Bath & Beyond

bedbathandbeyond.com
Shopping for bedsheets? Boring! But shopping
for race-car wheels and sponge-boat hulls? Now,
that's worth a trip. With so many departments from
bathroom to kitchen, this store is bound to have
something your kids will get excited to craft with!

IKEA

ikea.com
To know IKEA is to love IKEA, and their prices make
everything friendly for the DIYer.

Kelvin Educational

kelvin.com
A fantastic resource for your young engineers—here
you can get anything from wheels to rocket launch
pads.

Land of Nod

landofnod.com
An aspirational home collection for kids' rooms, their
furniture, accessories, wall art, and accents inspire a
creative atmosphere.

Lowe's

lowes.com
You don't really need to know what all of those wing
nuts and doodads do to know that they make amazing
craft supplies.

MISCELLANEOUS AND VINTAGE FINDS

eBay

ebay.com
Like an online flea market . . . you never know what
you'll find! I've gotten some great deals on old
buttons, crates, chandelier crystals, and vintage
wooden spools.

Etsy

etsy.com
When I'm in need of a random craft supply, Etsy is
the first place I look. And it's always there.

PAPER

Carte Fini Fine Italian Papers

cartefini.myshopify.com
With over fifty colors of crepe paper, you will never
shop for paper anywhere else again.

Paper Presentation

paperpresentation.com
Headquartered in Manhattan, this is the DIY mecca
for anything paper. I'm also addicted to their die-cut
colorful tags and printer labels.

Paper Source

papersource.com
Gorgeous paper and super-high-quality supplies.

PARTY SUPPLIES

Just Artifacts

justartifacts.net

A colorful mix of so many goodies. Paper straws, washi tape, paper lanterns, wool felt beads, mini clothespins . . . it's a treasure trove.

Shop Sweet Lulu

shopsweetlulu.com

If you want a well-curated party supply locale, Lulu is your lady! From striped paper straws to wooden demitasse spoons, you'll try your hardest to find a use for everything she sells.

RIBBON AND TRIM

M & J Trimming

mjtrim.com

Ribbon, beaded trim, leather cord, lace, buttons, sequins—I'm out of breath just thinking about this place.

Tinsel Trading

tinseltrading.com

This store full of ribbon, vintage beads, buttons, and baubles is so lovely and inspiring, you'll never want to leave.

TOYS

Melissa & Doug

melissaanddoug.com

The perfect toy companions to the crafts in this book; deck out your kids' play spaces with street signs, barns, baggage carriers, and parking garages.

YARN

Purl Soho

purlsoho.com

Their displays are like eye candy . . . full of gorgeous colors of yarns, threads, and fabrics, too. Everything is Instagram-worthy.

Acknowledgments

When people ask what I do for a living, I love that I can say "arts and crafts." But the truth is, bringing all of these creations to life in the form of a book is hard work! And the hard work isn't just my own—there are so many generous, kind, talented people who contribute their words, ideas, support, faces, and hands to the end product.

First to the unflappable, venerable, über-talented team at Artisan Books: Lia Ronnen, Bridget Monroe Itkin, Yeon Kim, Michelle Ishay-Cohen, Sibylle Kazeroid, Nancy Murray, Hanh Le, Allison McGeehon, and Breanne Sommer. This book exists because of your talent, your encouragement, and your belief that families want to experience crafts in a new way.

To the creative geniuses with whom I had the pleasure to work: my photographer, Alexandra Grablewski; my illustrator, Jordan Sondler; my wardrobe stylist, Jessica Zindren; my craft assistants, Lauren Krukowski and Dylan Wilde; and my photo assistants, Rebecca Lermsider and Jenna Tedesco.

Thank you to Michaels Stores for allowing me to represent your brand and for providing me the best tools of my trade. And many thanks to Oriental Trading for all the goodies I never knew I "needed."

To all of my friends, family, and colleagues who have supported me along the way: Ami Desai, Dan Schwartz, Traci Gingold, Jane Nussbaum, Micah Sommers, Judy Goldberg, Amanda Kirk, Scott Sternberg, Joel Bloom, Liz King, Jennifer Brett, Dena Cohen, Jack and Yvonne Cohen, Traci Gingold, Rachel Faucett, Danny Seo, Dana Points, Gabrielle Blair. And of course, my parents, Dan and Barbara Kingloff.

To all of the beautiful faces and patient hands (and their parents) that posed for this book: Jack Bloom, Chandra and Thalia Kyrwood, Aden Jobarteh, Shane Monfet, Sidney Levy, Elias Cortez, Sylvie Kunreuther, Rafael Carrillo, Jack Stanley, Kiran Yeh, Finley Frenkel, Sophia Kirk-Salazar, and Cecelia Vickers.

To my most precious "creations" ever . . . my children, Oliver and Sommer. Thank you for helping me prove that handmade crafts always win over digital devices.

And finally to Michael Cohen, my husband and partner in all things life, work, and craft. Your talents, creativity, and advice can be seen on every page of this book and beyond. Thank you for not kicking over my traffic light or punting my submarine as you tripped over them in the middle of the night.

The author and publisher wish to thank Land of Nod and Norman & Jules for providing beautiful props for use in this book, and the following companies for providing the adorable clothes: Appaman, Barque, CrewCuts, GapKids, H+M, Joah Love, Kapital K, Milk and Soda, Mim-Pi, Mini Boden, the Mini Classy, Neve/Hawk, Ode to Jeune, Old Navy, Peppercorn Kids, Pink Chicken, Target, Tuchinda, Velveteen, and Winkniks.